FREE DVD **FREE** FREE DVD

Essential Test Tips DVD from Trivium Test Prep

Dear Customer,

Thank you for purchasing from Cirrus Test Prep! Whether you're looking to join the military, get into college, or advance your career, we're honored to be a part of your journey.

To show our appreciation (and to help you relieve a little of that test-prep stress), we're offering a **FREE *TExES Essential Test Tips DVD**** by Cirrus Test Prep. Our DVD includes 35 test preparation strategies that will help keep you calm and collected before and during your big exam. All we ask is that you email us your feedback and describe your experience with our product. Amazing, awful, or just so-so: we want to hear what you have to say!

To receive your **FREE *TExES Essential Test Tips DVD***, please email us at 5star@ cirrustestprep.com. Include "Free 5 Star" in the subject line and the following information in your email:

1.   The title of the product you purchased.

2.   Your rating from 1 – 5 (with 5 being the best).

3.   Your feedback about the product, including how our materials helped you meet your goals and ways in which we can improve our products.

4.   Your full name and shipping address so we can send your **FREE *TExES Essential Test Tips DVD***.

If you have any questions or concerns please feel free to contact us directly at 5star@cirrustestprep.com.

Thank you, and good luck with your studies!

* Please note that the free DVD is <u>not included</u> with this book. To receive the free DVD, please follow the instructions above.

TExES History 7–12 Study Guide Rapid Review 2019–2020

TEST PREP AND PRACTICE QUESTIONS FOR THE TExES (233) EXAM

About the Authors

Alicia Chipman has taught history and social sciences in Chicago, Illinois since 2003. Having worked with both high school and junior high school students, Alicia has developed curricula to prepare students for AP exams and entrance into the International Baccalaureate diploma program. She is now Student Teacher Supervisor at the Chicago Center for Urban Life and Culture. She obtained her master's degree in Educational Policy at the University of Illinois Urbana-Champaign in 2013.

Caroline Brennan spent several years on the front lines of multilateral diplomacy at the United Nations, working with the International Committee of the Red Cross (ICRC) in humanitarian affairs from 2007 – 2012. Previously, she studied international development, postcolonial theory, and history in Canada, Europe, and North Africa; she obtained her master's degree from the University of Pennsylvania in 2007, specializing in Middle Eastern history.

Sandy Thomson is currently an instructor at Wright Career College and at Park University. She previously worked as a social studies teacher in Tulsa, Oklahoma in the Union Public Schools from 1997 – 2014, both online and in the traditional education program. She served as the Department Chair from 2009 – 2011.

Table of Contents

Online Resources

To help you fully prepare for your TExES History 7 – 12 (233) exam, Cirrus includes online resources with the purchase of this study guide.

PRACTICE TEST

In addition to the practice test included in this book, we also offer an online exam. Since many exams today are computer based, getting to practice your test-taking skills on the computer is a great way to prepare.

FLASH CARDS

A convenient supplement to this study guide, Cirrus's flash cards enable you to review important terms easily on your computer or smartphone.

CHEAT SHEETS

Review the skills you need to master the exam with easy-to-read Cheat Sheets.

FROM STRESS TO SUCCESS

Watch From Stress to Success, a brief but insightful YouTube video that offers the tips, tricks, and secrets experts use to score higher on the exam.

REVIEWS

Leave a review, send us helpful feedback, or sign up for Cirrus promotions—including free books!

Access these materials at:

www.cirrustestprep.com/texes-history-online-resources

Introduction

Congratulations on choosing to take the Texas Examination of Educational Standards (TExES) History 7 – 12 (233) Exam! By purchasing this book, you've taken a vital step toward becoming a history teacher.

This guide will provide you with a detailed overview of the TExES history, so you know exactly what to expect on test day. We'll take you through all the concepts covered on the test and give you the opportunity to test your knowledge with practice questions. Even if it's been a while since you last took a major test, don't worry; we'll make sure you're more than ready!

What is the TExES History?

TExES tests are a part of teaching certification in Texas. In conjunction with completion of an educator preparation program, TExES exam scores are used to complete a state application for teacher certification. The history exam ensures that the examinee has the skills and knowledge necessary to become an educator of history in Texas public schools.

What's on the TExES History?

The TExES is a 100-question, multiple-choice test designed to assess whether you possess the knowledge and skills necessary to become a history educator in the state of Texas. The test's content covers four domains, or concepts, that are illustrated in the following table; the number of questions specific to each domain is approximate. You have a maximum of five hours to complete the test.

TExES History 7 – 12 (233)		
Domain	**Approximate Number of Questions per Subject**	**Percentage**
World History	30	30%
US History	36	36%
Texas History	20	20%
Social Studies Foundations, Skills, Research, and Instruction	14	14%
Total	**100 (always)**	**5 hours**

You will answer approximately thirty multiple-choice questions on world history. In general, you will be expected to understand how world societies and civilizations have been shaped by conflict, technology, and religion; ideologies like nationalism, totalitarianism and other political philosophies; economic movements like industrialization and the market economy; and major demographic trends. The test will also presume an understanding of trans-global similarities in gender and family expectations and the impact of trade within and among cultures. Specific questions may ask about the classical civilizations in Europe and Asia and their transformation from 300 – 1400 CE; European developments from the Renaissance through the Enlightenment; colonization, trade, and other global interactions from 1200–1750 CE; the consequences of nationalism and European imperialism from 1750 – 1914 CE; the causes and consequences of the First and Second World Wars (like decolonization and the rise of the Soviet Union); and the important developments of the post-Cold War world (such as globalization and fundamentalism).

You will answer approximately thirty-six multiple-choice questions on United States history. The test will require knowledge of North American geography, pre-colonial civilizations, the purposes of European colonization of the continent, and how pre-colonial peoples interacted with European colonizers. Be prepared for questions about the American Revolution and the foundations of the United States government and Constitution. The test will cover developments in the nineteenth century, including westward expansion, political division, the Civil War, Reconstruction, industrialization, urbanization, and immigration. The Progressive Era and the New Deal are covered as well. Be aware not only of United States involvement in the First and Second World Wars, but also of their impact on both foreign and domestic policy. Prepare for thematic questions that will test your knowledge of the impact of labor and technology on the economy, changing political trends from the New Deal and Great Society to conservatism, the impact of religion on society, and civil rights and changing perceptions of race, ethnicity and gender roles throughout the twentieth century. Questions are also likely to explore the

United States' emergence and role as a world power during the Cold War and into the twenty-first century.

You will answer approximately twenty multiple-choice questions on Texas history. The test will require an understanding of significant events and developments in Texas history through the beginning of the Mexican National Era in 1821 to the present. Be prepared for questions that discuss the early history of Texas from the Spanish Colonial Era to the Mexican National Era; questions may address American Indian groups, European exploration, and Spanish colonialism. The test will cover important events, individuals, and issues related to Texas expansion and settlement, the Texas Revolution, the Republic of Texas and early statehood, the US Civil War, and Reconstruction in Texas. Questions will also explore ideas and individuals from the Progressive and Civil Rights movements and major social, economic, and political events of the twentieth and twenty-first centuries. Prepare for questions about major developments in the petroleum and gas industry, manufacturing, commercial agriculture, and suburbanization. You should also understand the significance and impact of geographic features and major economic and cultural developments throughout Texas and its history.

You will answer approximately fourteen multiple-choice questions on social studies foundation, skills, research, and instruction. Expect questions regarding instructional practice and state performance standards that comprise Texas Essential Knowledge and Skills (TEKS) in social studies. You will also be expected to correctly use social studies terminology and understand the foundation and impact of social studies as a discipline. Furthermore, questions will test your ability to interpret and communicate social studies information in various forms: for example, by correctly utilizing primary and secondary sources.

How is the TExES Scored?

On the TExES, the number of correctly answered questions are used to create your scaled score. Scores are scaled to a number in the range 100 – 300, a passing score being 240. The score shows your performance on the test as a whole and is scaled to allow comparison across various versions of the tests. There is no penalty for guessing on TExES tests, so be sure to eliminate answer choices and answer every question. If you still do not know the answer, guess; you may get it right! Keep in mind that about twenty multiple-choice questions are experimental questions for the purpose of the TExES test-makers and will not count toward your overall score. However, as those questions are not indicated on the test, you must respond to every question.

Your score report will be available online through your ETS account two to three weeks after your testing date. Scores are automatically made available to TEA and EPP, so you do not have to manually report your scores.

How is the TExES Administered?

TExES exams are administered at testing centers throughout Texas and the United States. Check http://cms.texes-ets.org/cat/testcenters/ for a testing center near you. The TExES history exam is a computerized test offered continuously throughout the year. After you set up an account at http://cms.texes-ets.org/youraccount/, you can locate testing centers, register for a test, or find instructions for registering via mail or phone.

On the day of your test, be sure to bring your admission ticket (which is available on your ETS account) and valid photo ID. You are allowed no personal effects in the testing area. Cell phones and other electronic, photographic, recording, or listening devices are not permitted in the testing center at all, and bringing those items may be cause for dismissal, forfeiture of your testing fees, and cancellation of your scores. For details on to expect at your testing center, refer to http://cms.texes-ets.org/texes/dayofthetest/day-test-general-guidelines/.

About Cirrus Test Prep

Cirrus Test Prep study guides are designed by current and former educators and are tailored to meet your needs as an incoming educator. Our guides offer all of the resources necessary to help you pass teacher certification tests across the nation.

Cirrus clouds are graceful, wispy clouds characterized by their high altitude. Just like cirrus clouds, Cirrus Test Prep's goal is to help educators "aim high" when it comes to obtaining their teacher certification and entering the classroom.

About This Guide

This guide will help you master the most important test topics and also develop critical test-taking skills. We have built features into our books to prepare you for your tests and increase your score. Along with a detailed summary of the test's format, content, and scoring, we offer an in-depth overview of the content knowledge required to pass the test. Our sidebars provide interesting information, highlight key concepts, and review content so that you can solidify your understanding of the exam's concepts. Test your knowledge with sample questions and detailed answer explanations in the text that help you think through the problems on the exam and two full-length practice tests that reflect the content and format of the TExES. We're pleased you've chosen Cirrus to be a part of your professional journey.

World History

EARLY CIVILIZATIONS AND THE GREAT EMPIRES

PALEOLITHIC AND NEOLITHIC ERAS

The earliest humans were hunter-gatherers until the development of agriculture in about 11,000 BCE. 60,000–70,000 years ago, early humans began migrating from Africa, gradually spreading out across the continents.

Early human history begins with the **Paleolithic** era. During this period, early **hominids** like our ancestors *Homo sapiens sapiens* and *Homo neanderthalensis* exhibited the use of rudimentary tools based on stone, before metalworking. Hence, the term *Stone Age* describes this period.

From approximately 11,000–10,500 BCE, humans started settled communities, developed agricultural practices, and began domesticating animals. They also started using metal to make tools, weapons, and other objects. This was the beginning of the **Neolithic** period, characterized by behavioral and technological change like the invention of the wheel. During the **Bronze Age**, humans began working with copper and tin, creating stronger tools and weapons.

MIDDLE EAST AND EGYPT

Settled societies organized into larger centralized communities characterized by early social stratification and rule of law. The earliest known examples of these were in the **Fertile Crescent**, the area in North Africa and Southwest Asia stretching from Egypt through the Levant and into Mesopotamia.

Around 2500 BCE the **Sumerians** emerged in the Near East. Developing irrigation and advanced agriculture, they were able to develop city-states. They also invented **cuneiform**, the first alphabet, which allowed advanced governance and administration. Sumer featured city-states, the potter's wheel, early astronomy and mathematics, literature, and religious thought.

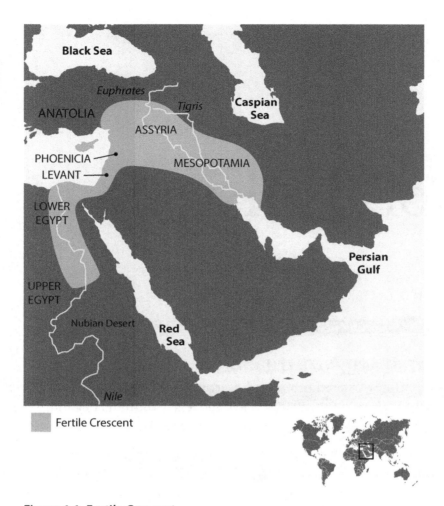

Figure 1.1. Fertile Crescent

Eventually the Sumerians were overcome by Semitic-speaking, nomadic peoples in the Fertile Crescent: the result was the **Akkadian Empire**. Around the eighteenth century BCE, the Akkadians had given way to **Babylonia** in Southern Mesopotamia and **Assyria** in the north. These two civilizations would develop roughly concurrently.

Assyria had developed as a powerful city-state in northern Mesopotamia. Influenced by the Sumerians and Akkadians, the Assyrians developed unique sculpture and jewelry, established regional military dominance, and played an important role in regional trade. At odds with Babylonia over the centuries, the Assyrian Empire had grown to encompass most of the Fertile Crescent.

Like Assyria, Babylonia inherited elements of Akkadian and Sumerian civilization. By the eighteenth century BCE, King Hammurabi in Babylonia had developed courts and an early codified rule of law—**the Code of Hammurabi**—which meted out justice on an equal basis: "an eye for an eye, a tooth for a tooth."

Babylonia continued urban development supported by organized agriculture, warfare, administration, and justice; Babylon became a major ancient city. Babylonia developed more advanced astronomy, medicine, mathematics, philosophy, art, and literature like the *Epic of Gilgamesh*.

Around 1200 BCE Mesopotamia became vulnerable to the **Hittites** from Anatolia. The Hittites had developed in the Bronze Age but flourished in the **Iron Age**, developing expertise in metallurgy to create strong weapons; they also mastered horsemanship and invented chariots. Thus the Hittites became a strong military power and a threat to regional empires and their commercial interests.

> **DID YOU KNOW?**
>
> Settled communities needed the reliable sources of food and fresh water a temperate climate could provide. Surpluses of food allowed for cultural and civilizational development, not just survival.

Meanwhile, development had been under way in the **Nile Valley** in ancient **Egypt**. Known for their pyramids, art, and pictorial writing (**hieroglyphs**), the ancient Egyptians emerged as early as 5000 BCE; evidence of Egyptian unity under one monarch, or **pharaoh**, dates to the First Dynasty, around 3000 BCE.

Despite the surrounding Sahara Desert, the land along the Nile River was arable. Irrigation enabled the Egyptians to develop settled communities. Civilizations emerged on the Upper and Lower Nile, unifying under the early dynasties led by pharaohs, with the Egyptian capital at **Memphis**.

By the fourth dynasty, Egypt's civilizational institutions, written language, art, and architecture were well developed. It was during this period that the famous **pyramids** were erected at Giza as burial tombs. In addition, the complex religious mythology of ancient Egypt had become established. Egypt grew in power from 1550 to 1290 BCE. Led by the powerful Pharaoh **Thutmose III**, Egypt expanded into the Levant.

Later, **King Akhenaten (Amenhotep IV)** abolished the Egyptian religion, establishing a cult of the sun linked to himself. During this period Egypt saw a surge of iconoclastic art and sculpture. However, his successors returned to traditional values. Under **Ramesses II**, Egypt battled the Hittites in the Levant, reaching a stalemate. Egypt fell into decline, losing control of the Levant and eventually falling to Assyria.

> **QUICK REVIEW**
>
> What were the contributions of the early Middle Eastern civilizations? List several.

INDIA

Meanwhile, early civilizations also developed farther east. The **Indus Valley Civilizations** flourished in the Indian Subcontinent and the Indus and Ganges river basins. The **Harappan** civilization was based in Punjab from around 3000 BCE. The major cities of **Harappa** and **Mohenjo-daro** featured grid systems indicative of detailed urban planning; they may be the earliest planned cities in the world. In addition, Harappan objects found in Mesopotamia reveal trade links between these civilizations.

Later, concurrent with the Roman Empire, the **Gupta Empire** emerged in India. During this period, the Golden Age of India, the region was economically strong. Oceanic trade flourished with China, East Africa, and the Middle East in spices, ivory, silk, cotton, and iron, which was highly profitable as an export.

The Guptas encouraged music, art, architecture, and Sanskrit literature and philosophy. While practitioners of Hinduism, the empire was tolerant of Buddhists and Jains. Organized administration and rule of law made it possible for **Chandragupta II** to govern a large territory throughout the Subcontinent. However, by 550 BCE, invasions from the north by the Huns and internal conflicts within the Subcontinent led to imperial decline.

CHINA

In China, the **Shang dynasty**, the first known dynasty, ruled the **Huang He** or **Yellow River** area around the second millennium BCE and developed the earliest known Chinese writing. Like the early civilizations in the Middle East, the Shang dynasty featured the use of bronze technology, horses, wheeled technology, walled cities, and other developments.

Around 1056 BCE the **Zhou** dynasty emerged and China expanded to the **Chiang Jiang** (Yangtze River) region. Family aristocracies controlled the country in a hierarchy similar to later European feudalism, setting the foundation for hierarchical rule and social stratification.

The concept of the **Mandate of Heaven**, in which the emperor had a divine mandate to rule, emerged. The unstable period toward the end of the Zhou dynasty was known as the **Spring and Autumn Period**; during this time **Confucius** lived (c. 551–479 BCE). His teachings would be the basis for Confucianism, the foundational Chinese philosophy emphasizing harmony and respect for hierarchy.

Following the chaotic **Warring States Period** (c. 475–221 BCE) the short-lived but influential **Qin dynasty** emerged, unifying disparate Chinese civilizations and regions under the first emperor, **Qin Shihuangdi**. This dynasty (221–206 BCE) was characterized by expanded infrastructure, standardization in weights and measures, writing, and currency. The administrative **bureaucracy** established by the emperor was the foundation of Chinese administration until the twentieth century.

DID YOU KNOW?

Shared customs like the use of silkworms, jade, chopsticks, and the practice of Confucianism also indicated early Chinese unity.

Figure 1.2. Great Wall of China

In addition, the emperor constructed the **Great Wall of China**, and his tomb is guarded by the famous **terracotta figurines**. During the Qin dynasty, China expanded as far south as Vietnam.

The **Han dynasty** took over in 206 for the next 300 years (206 BCE–220 CE), retaining Qin administrative organization and adding Confucian ideals of hierarchy and harmony.

THE AMERICAS

Prehistoric peoples migrated to the Americas from Asia during the Paleolithic period, and evidence of their presence dates to at least 13,000 years ago.

From around 1200 BCE, the **Olmec** civilization developed on the Mexican Gulf Coast. Its massive sculptures reflect complex religious and spiritual beliefs. Later civilizations in Mexico included the **Zapotecs**, **Mixtecs**, **Toltecs**, and **Mayas** in the Yucatán peninsula, developing irrigation to expand agriculture.

Meanwhile, in South America, artistic evidence remains of the **Chavin**, **Moche**, and **Nazca** peoples, who preceded the later Inca civilization and empire. The Chavin style influenced later Andean art. The construction of the Nazca lines, enormous sketches engraved in the ground, remains a mystery.

In North America, the ancient mounds in the Mississippi region may be ancient spiritual structures. Precolonial North American peoples are discussed in the US history chapter.

PERSIA AND GREECE

The **Persian** emperor **Cyrus** conquered the Babylonians in the sixth century BCE. His son **Darius** extended Persian rule from the Indus Valley to Egypt, and north to Anatolia by about 400 BCE, where the Persians encountered the ancient Greeks. **Greek** (or Hellenic) culture impacted the development of European civilization.

Greece was comprised of city-states like **Athens**, the first known **democracy**, and the military state **Sparta**. Historically these city-states had been rivals; however, they temporarily united against Persia. It was during this period, the **Golden Age** of Greek civilization, that much of the Hellenic art, architecture, and philosophy known today emerged.

QUICK REVIEW

How is Greek philosophy relevant today?

The term *democracy* comes from the Greek word *demokratia*—"people power." It was participatory rather than representative; officials were chosen by groups rather than elected.

In this period and into the fourth century BCE, the **Parthenon** was built, as were other characteristic examples of ancient Greek sculpture and architecture. **Socrates** began teaching, influencing later philosophers like **Plato** and **Aristotle** who established the basis for modern western philosophical and political thought.

Despite its status as a democracy, Athens was not fully democratic: women did not have a place in politics, and Athenians practiced slavery. Furthermore, those men eligible to participate in political life had to prove that both of their parents were Athenian (the criterion of double descent).

Toward the end of the fifth century BCE, Athens and Sparta were at odds during the **Peloponnesian War** (431–404 BCE), which ultimately crippled the Athenian democracy permanently. Later in the fourth century BCE, Philip II of Macedonia was able to take over most of Greece. His son **Alexander** (later known as Alexander the Great) proceded to conquer Persia, spreading Greek civilization throughout Western and Central Asia.

ROME

Meanwhile, in Italy, the ancient Romans were consolidating their power. The city of **Rome** was founded by the eighth century BCE; it became strong thanks to its importance as a trade route for the Greeks and other Mediterranean peoples. Early Roman culture drew from the **Etruscans**, inhabitants of the Italian peninsula, and the Greeks, from whom it borrowed elements of architecture, art, language, and even religion.

Rome became a republic in 509 BCE and elected lawmakers (senators) to the **Senate**. The Romans developed highly advanced infrastructure and began conquering areas around the Mediterranean, expanding to North Africa.

With conquest of territory and expansion of trade came increased slavery, and working class Romans (**Plebeians**) were displaced; at the same time, the wealthy ruling class (**Patricians**) became more powerful and corrupt. Resulting protest movements led to legislative reform and republican stabilization, strengthening the republic by the first century BCE.

While militarily and economically strong, the republic was increasingly divided between the wealthy ruling class (the **Optimates**) and the discontented working, poor, and military class (the **Populare**). The Senate weakened due to its own corruption, and the leaders **Julius Caesar**, **Pompey**, and **Crassus** took control in a short-lived triumvirate.

Caesar took over and began to transition Rome from a republic to an empire. Caesar was assassinated by a group of senators in 44 BCE; however, in that short time he had been able to consolidate and centralize imperial control. His nephew **Octavian** eventually took control of Rome in 31 BCE. He took the name **Augustus Caesar**, becoming the first Roman emperor.

At this time, Rome reached the height of its power, and the empire enjoyed a period of stability known as the *Pax Romana.* Rome controlled the entire Mediterranean region and lands stretching as far north as Germany and Britain, territory into the Balkans, far into the Middle East, Egypt, North Africa, and Iberia.

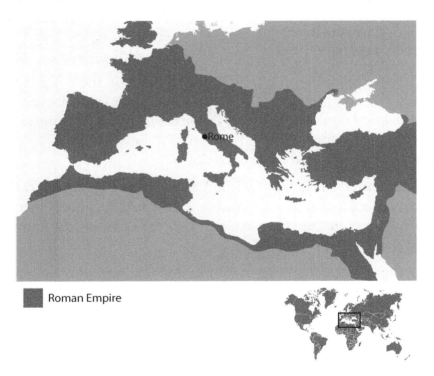

■ Roman Empire

Figure 1.3. Pax Romana

In this time of relative peace and prosperity, Latin literature flourished, as did art, architecture, philosophy, mathematics, science, and international trade throughout Rome and beyond into Asia and Africa. A series of emperors would follow and Rome remained a major world power, but it would never again reach the height of prosperity and stability that it did under Augustus.

It was during the time of Augustus that a Jewish carpenter named Jesus in Palestine began teaching that he was the son of the Jewish God, and that his death would provide salvation for all of humanity. Jesus was eventually crucified; followers of **Jesus Christ**, called Christians, preached his teachings of redemption throughout Rome. Despite the persecution faced by early Christians, **Christianity**'s universal appeal and applicability to people of diverse backgrounds would allow it to spread quickly.

By 300 CE, Rome was in decline. The Christian emperor **Constantine** moved the capital to **Constantinople** and established Christianity as an official religion. The balance of power and stability shifted to the east.

This political shift enabled the western (later, Catholic) church to gain power in Rome. Over time, the Catholic Church would become one of the most powerful political entities in the world; today, there are around one billion Catholics worldwide.

DID YOU KNOW?
These clans and others from Central Asia were able to defeat the Romans in the north and settle in Europe, thanks to their equestrian skills, superior wheels, and iron technology.

The western part of the Roman Empire gradually fell into disarray and succumbed to invading European clans like the **Anglo-Saxons**, the **Franks**, the **Visigoths**, the **Ostrogoths**, and the **Slavs**. The last emperor was killed in Rome in **476 CE**, marking the end of the empire.

Meanwhile the eastern part of the Roman Empire, with its capital at Constantinople, evolved into the **Byzantine Empire**. The Byzantine emperor **Justinian** (527 – 565 CE) reconquered parts of North Africa, Egypt, and Greece, established rule of law, and reinvigorated trade with China.

He also nurtured Christianity, building the **Hagia Sophia**, the cathedral and center of orthodox Christianity. Over time, a clear schism would emerge between the church in Rome and Christians in Constantinople, creating the Roman Catholic Church and the Greek Orthodox Church.

During the early Middle Ages in Europe and the Byzantine Empire, the roots of another civilization were developing in the Arabian Peninsula. In the seventh century, the Prophet **Muhammad** began teaching **Islam**. Based on the teachings of Judaism and Christianity and following the same god, Islam presented as the final version of these two religions. Like Christianity, it held universal appeal.

SAMPLE QUESTIONS

1) **What is required for a settled community?**

   A. domesticated animals
    B. a source of fresh water
   C. technology
   D. weapons

   Answer:

   B. Correct. Fresh water permits a reliable food source, which allows for settlement; people need not travel in search of food.

2) **The earliest known form of alphabetic writing (using characters to create words) is**

   A. cuneiform, developed by the Egyptians.
    B. cuneiform, developed by the Sumerians.
   C. hieroglyphs, developed by the Egyptians.
   D. hieroglyphs, developed by the Sumerians.

   Answer:

   B. Correct. The Sumerians developed cuneiform. Hieroglyphs are pictographs.

3) **The Shang and Zhou dynasties are particularly relevant in Chinese history for their contributions in**

   A. developing Chinese administration.
   B. centralizing Chinese imperial power as symbolized through the terracotta figurines in the imperial tombs.
   C. forming a Chinese identity through the development of written language, the Emperor's Mandate of Heaven, and fostering Confucianism.
   D. ensuring China's safety by building the Great Wall of China.

   Answer:

   C. Correct. Written Chinese developed under the Shang dynasty, and the Mandate of Heaven emerged under the Zhou dynasty; furthermore, other cultural traditions emerged during these periods.

4)   **The Athenian concept of democracy embraced**

    A.   participatory democracy, in which local groups made decisions directly by vote.

    B.   an anonymous electoral process similar to that of the United States in which officials were elected.

    C.   people of all backgrounds, so that all residents of Athens had a stake in the political process.

    D.   an educated electorate in order to ensure the best possible decision-making.

Answer:

    A.   Correct. The Athenian notion of *demokratia*, or people power, was participatory rather than representative.

5)   **How did Julius Caesar rise to and retain power?**

    A.   He invaded Rome with his armies from Gaul, and used his military resources to control the empire.

    B.   He was elected president of the Senate by the people thanks to widespread political support.

    C.   He took control of the Senate thanks to his charisma and popularity among the people.

    D.   As part of the Triumvirate, he was guaranteed a leadership position.

Answer:

    C.   Correct. The Senate's corruption and weakness, and Caesar's popularity with the Populare, enabled him to take and retain control.

FEUDALISM THROUGH THE ERA OF EXPANSION

THE MIDDLE AGES IN EUROPE

The Byzantine Empire remained a strong civilization. Constantinople was a commercial center, strategically located at the Dardanelles, connecting Asian trade routes with Europe. Later, missionaries traveled north to Slavic Russia, spreading Christianity and literacy. Russian Christianity was influenced by Byzantine doctrine, what would become Greek Orthodox Christianity.

Despite the chaos in Western Europe, the church in Rome remained strong, becoming a stabilizing influence. However, differences in doctrine between Rome and Constantinople became too wide to overcome. Beginning in 1054, a series of **schisms** developed between the two. Eventually two entirely separate churches emerged: the **Roman Catholic Church** and the **Greek Orthodox Church**.

In Europe, the early Middle Ages (or *Dark Ages*) from the fall of Rome to about the tenth century, were a chaotic and unsafe time. What protection and stability existed were represented and maintained by the Catholic Church and the feudal system.

Society and economics were characterized by decentralized, local governance, or **feudalism**, a hierarchy where land and protection were offered in exchange for loyalty. Feudalism was the dominant social, economic, and political hierarchy of the European Middle Ages.

In exchange for protection, **vassals** would pledge **fealty**, or **pay homage** to **lords**. Lords were landowners who rewarded their vassals' loyalty with land, or **fiefs**, and protection. Economic and social organization revolved around **manors**, self-sustaining areas possessed by lords but worked by peasants. The peasants were **serfs**. Tied to the land, they worked for the lord in exchange for protection; however they were not obligated to fight. Usually they were also granted some land for their own use. While not true slaves, their lives were effectively controlled by the lord.

Warriors who fought for lords, called **knights**, were rewarded with land and could become lords in their own right. Lords themselves were vassals of other lords; that hierarchy extended upward to kings or the Catholic Church. The Catholic Church itself was a major landowner and political power. In a Europe not yet dominated by sovereign states, the **Pope** was not only a religious leader, but also a military and political one.

Small kingdoms were scattered throughout Europe, and stable trade was difficult to maintain. One exception to the chaos was the Scandinavian **Viking** civilization. From the end of the eighth century until around 1100, the Vikings expanded from Scandinavia thanks to their seafaring skills and technology. The Vikings traded with the Byzantine Empire and European powers. They traveled to and raided parts of Britain, Ireland, France, and Russia.

DID YOU KNOW?

There were limits on sovereign power. In 1215, English barons forced King John to sign the Magna Carta, which protected their property and rights and is the basis of Britain's current parliamentary system.

Meanwhile, by the eighth century the North African **Moors**, part of the expanding Islamic civilization, had entered Iberia and were a threat to Christian Europe. **Charles Martel**, leader of the **Franks** in what is today France, defeated the Moors in 732 CE, stopping further Islamic incursion into Europe. Instability followed Charles Martel's death, however, and **Charlemagne**, the son of a court official, eventually took over the Franks.

Charlemagne was able to maintain Frankish unity, extend Frankish control into Central Europe, and protect the **Papal States** in central Italy. Parts of Western and Central Europe became organized under Charlemagne, who was crowned emperor of the Roman Empire by Pope Leo III in 800 CE. While in retrospect this seems long after the end of Rome, at the time many Europeans still perceived themselves as still part of a Roman Empire. Today Charlemagne's rule is referred to as the **Carolingian Empire**.

Charlemagne brought stability to Western and Central Europe during a period when two powerful, non-Christian, organized civilizations—the Vikings in the north and the Islamic powers in the south—threatened what was left of western Christendom, and when insecurity was growing to the east with the decline of the Byzantines and the emergence of the Islamic Umayyad Caliphate in Damascus. His reign strengthened the Roman Catholic Church and enabled a resurgence of Roman and Christian scholarship.

It was also under Charlemagne that the feudal system became truly organized, bringing more stability to Western Europe. In 962 CE, **Otto I** became emperor of the **Holy Roman Empire** in Central Europe, a confederation of small states which remained an important European power until its dissolution in 1806.

In 1066, **William the Conqueror** left Normandy in northwest France. The **Normans** established feudalism, Christianity, and economic organization in England. Intermarriage and conquest resulted in English control of parts of France, too. Conflict between Britain and France would continue for several centuries, while rulers in Scandinavia and Northwest Europe consolidated power.

THE ISLAMIC WORLD AND CHINA

Meanwhile, in the wake of the decline of the Byzantine Empire, **Arab-Islamic empires**, characterized by brisk commerce, advancements in technology and learning, and urban development, arose in the Middle East.

Before the rise of Islam in the seventh century, the Arabian Peninsula was located at the intersection of the Byzantine Empire, and the **Sasanians** (Persians), who practiced **Zoroastrianism**. Both of these empires sought to control trade with Central and eastern Asia along the Silk Road as well as with Christian Axum (Ethiopia).

In Arabia itself, Judaism, Christianity, and animist religions were practiced by the Arab majority. The Prophet **Muhammad** was born in Mecca around 570; he began receiving messages from God (Allah), writing them as the **Qur'an**, the Islamic holy book. He preached the religion of **Islam** around 613 as the last, most correct version of the monotheistic religions. Driven from **Mecca** to Medina in 622, Muhammad and his followers recaptured the city and other major Arabian towns by the time of his death, establishing Islam and Arab rule in the region.

Islam appealed to many in the disorganized region. The religion's demands (the **Five Pillars of Islam**) asked followers to declare faith in one god (Allah), pray five times daily, donate 10 percent of their earnings to the community, make a pilgrimage at least once in their lifetimes to Mecca, and fast during the holy month of Ramadan. Anyone could easily convert to the religion, and it brought stability and social organization to a chaotic region and time.

DID YOU KNOW?

A caliph was considered both a political and a religious leader.

After Muhammad's death in **632 CE**, his followers went on to conquer land north into the weakening Byzantine Empire. The Muslim Arabs led incursions into Syria, the Levant, and Mesopotamia, taking over these territories. Thanks to military, bureaucratic, and organizational skill as well as their ability to win over dissatisfied minorities, the Arabs eventually isolated the Byzantines to parts of Anatolia and Constantinople and crushed the Persian Sasanians.

However, disagreements over leadership led to conflict among Muslims and the Sunni-Shi'a Schism. The **Shi'ites**, who centered in Mesopotamia, believed that Muhammad's cousin Ali was the rightful heir to the early Islamic empire. The followers of the Meccan elites became known as **Sunnis**, "orthodox" Muslims with a focus on community rather than genealogy. Over the centuries, other differences would develop.

The **Umayyad Caliphate** (empire), based in Damascus, was named for the leading Meccan tribe that had supported Muhammad from the beginning. By 750, the Arabs would control land from North Africa to the Indus River Valley and Spain (al-Andalus).

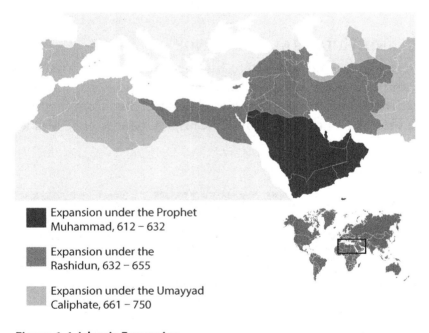

Expansion under the Prophet Muhammad, 612 – 632

Expansion under the Rashidun, 632 – 655

Expansion under the Umayyad Caliphate, 661 – 750

Figure 1.4. Islamic Expansion

Ongoing conflict among Arab elites resulted in the **Abbasid Caliphate** in 750 CE. The Umayyads were overthrown by the Arab-Muslim Abbasid family, which established a new capital in Baghdad. The Abbasids professionalized the military, helping consolidate imperial control and improving tax collection.

The administration and stability provided by the caliphates fostered an Arabic literary culture. Stability permitted open trade routes, economic development, and cultural interaction throughout Asia, the Middle East, North Africa, and parts of Europe.

Thanks to the universality of the Arabic language, scientific and medical texts from varying civilizations—Greek, Persian, Indian—could be translated into Arabic and shared throughout the Islamic world. Arab thinkers studied Greek and Persian astronomy and engaged in further research. Arabs studied mathematics from around the world and developed algebra, enabling engineering, technological, artistic, and architectural achievements.

Around this time, the **Song dynasty (960–1276)** controlled most of China. Under the Song, China experienced tremendous development and economic growth. Characterized by increasing urbanization, the Song featured complex administrative rule, including the difficult competitive written examinations required to obtain prestigious bureaucratic positions in government.

Most traditions recognized as Chinese emerged under the Song, including the consumption of tea and rice and common Chinese architecture. The Song engaged not only in overland trade along the Silk Road, exporting silk, tea, ceramics, jade, and other goods, but also sea trade with Korea, Japan, Southeast Asia, India, Arabia, and even East Africa.

CONFLICT AND CULTURAL EXCHANGE

Cultural exchange was not limited to interactions among Christian Europeans, Egyptians, and Levantine Muslims. International commerce was vigorous along the **Silk Road,** the term for trading routes which stretched from the Arab-controlled Eastern Mediterranean to Song dynasty China, where science and learning also blossomed.

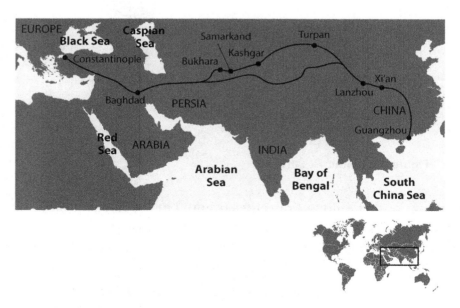

Figure 1.5. The Silk Road

The Silk Road reflected the transnational nature of Central Asia. The nomadic culture of Central Asia lent itself to trade among the major civilizations of China, Persia, the Near East, and Europe. Buddhism and Islam spread into China. Chinese, Islamic, and European art, pottery, and goods were interchanged among the three civilizations—early globalization. The Islamic hajj (the pilgrimage to Mecca) spurred cultural interaction, too.

QUICK REVIEW

How did the Silk Road and Islam *both* contribute to global cultural exchange?

Islam also spread along trans-Saharan trade routes into West Africa and the Sahel. Brisk trade between the gold-rich **Kingdom of Ghana** and Muslim traders based in Morocco brought Islam to the region around the eleventh century. The Islamic **Mali Empire** (1235–1500), based farther south in **Timbuktu**, eventually extended beyond the original Ghanaian boundaries to the West African coast and controlled the valuable gold and salt trades. It became a center of learning and commerce. However, by 1500, the **Songhai Empire** had overcome Mali and dominated the Niger River area.

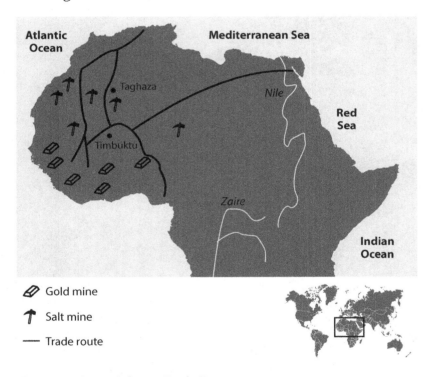

Figure 1.6. Trans-Saharan Trade Routes

Loss of Byzantine territory to the Islamic empires meant loss of Christian lands in the Levant to Muslims. In 1095, the Byzantine Emperor asked **Pope Urban II** for help to defend Jerusalem and protect Christians there. European Christians were easily inspired to fight in what became known as the **First Crusade**. The pope offered lords and knights the chance to keep lands and bounty they conquered. He also offered Crusaders **indulgences**—forgiveness for sins committed in war and guarantees they would enter heaven.

Meanwhile, towards the end of the tenth century, the Abbasid Caliphate was in decline. The Shi'ite **Fatimids** took control of Syria and Egypt, addressing the Shi'ite claim to the caliphate. Other groups took control of provinces in Mesopotamia, Arabia, Spain, and Central Asia.

Figure 1.7. Great Mosque Cordoba

Despite conflict in Europe, Christians found they had more in common with each other than with Muslims and united to fight in the Middle East. The decline of the Abbasids had left the Levant vulnerable, and Christian Crusaders established settlements and small kingdoms in Syria and on the eastern Mediterranean coast, conquering major cities and capturing Jerusalem by 1099.

The Crusades continued over several centuries. The Kurdish military leader **Salah al-Din** (Saladin) defeated the Fatimids in Egypt and reconquered Jerusalem in 1187, driving European Christians out for good. Following Salah al-Din's death, the **Mamluks (1250–1517)** controlled Egypt.

> **DID YOU KNOW?**
>
> During the Hundred Years' War, Joan of Arc led the French in the 1429 Battle of Orléans, inspiring French resistance to the English.

While the Crusades never resulted in permanent European control over the Holy Land, they did open up trade routes between Europe and the Middle East, stretching all the way along the Silk Road to China. This increasing interdependence led to the European Renaissance.

Ongoing interactions between Europeans and Muslims exposed Europeans, who could now afford them thanks to international trade, to improved education and goods. However, the **Bubonic (Black) Plague** also spread to Europe as a result of global exchange, killing off a third of its population from 1347–1351. The plague had a worldwide impact: empires fell in its wake.

Back in Europe, conflict reached its height throughout the thirteenth and fourteenth centuries: the **Hundred Years' War** (1337–1453). France was in political chaos, decentralized and at times without a king; suffering the effects of the Black Plague; vulnerable to English attack; and periodically under English rule. While conflict would continue, England lost its last territory in France, Bordeaux, in 1453.

> **DID YOU KNOW?**
>
> Ferdinand and Isabella launched the Inquisition, an extended persecution of Jews and Jewish converts to Christianity who continued to practice Judaism in secret. Muslims were also persecuted and forced to convert to Christianity or be exiled.

In Spain, despite some coexistence between Christians and Muslims under Muslim rule, raids and conflict were ongoing during the lengthy period of the Christian **Reconquista** of Iberia, which did not end until 1492 when Christian powers took Grenada, uniting Spain.

EMPIRES IN TRANSITION

Beyond Egypt and the Levant, the collapse of the Abbasid Caliphate led to instability and decentralization of power in Mesopotamia, Persia, and Central Asia; smaller sultanates (territories ruled by sultans, regional leaders) emerged, and production and economic development declined. **Tang dynasty** China closed its borders and trade on the Silk Road declined. In the eleventh century, the nomadic Seljuks dominated the region from Central Asia through parts of the Levant. However, the Seljuks lacked effective administration or central authority.

Islam remained a unifying force throughout the region, and political instability and decentralization paradoxically allowed local culture to develop, particularly Persian art and literature. Furthermore, Islam was able to thrive during this period: local religious leaders (**ulama**) had taken up community leadership positions, and Islam became a guiding force in law, justice, and social organization. Yet political decentralization ultimately left the region vulnerable to the Mongol invasions of the twelfth and thirteenth centuries.

> **DID YOU KNOW?**
>
> During this period, Persian-influenced Sufi (mystical) Islam and poetry developed; Shi'ite theology and jurisprudence also developed as part of a strengthening independent Shi'ite identity.

In the Near East, the **Mongol invasions** destroyed agriculture, city life and planning, economic patterns and trade routes, and social stability. After some time, new patterns of trade emerged, new cities rose to prominence, and stability allowed prosperity, but the Mongol invasions dealt a blow to confidence in Islam.

Likewise, in China, the Mongols destroyed local infrastructure, including the foundation of Chinese society and administration—the civil service examinations. However, in order to govern the vast territory effectively, the Mongols in China took a different approach. Genghis Khan's grandson **Kublai Khan** conquered China and founded the Mongol **Yuan dynasty** in 1271, maintaining administrative infrastructure and education in the Confucian tradition.

Mongol attempts at imperial expansion in China into Japan and Southeast Asia, coupled with threats from the Black Plague, financial problems, and flooding, led to the decline of the Yuan dynasty and the rise of the Han Chinese **Ming dynasty** in 1368. The Ming reasserted Han Chinese control and continued traditional methods of administration; however the construction of the **Forbidden City**, the home of the Emperor in Beijing, helped consolidate imperial rule. The Ming also encouraged international trade.

Mongol decline was not only isolated to China; in Russia, **Ivan the Great** brought Moscow from Mongol to Slavic Russian control. In the late fifteenth century, Ivan had consolidated Russian power over neighboring Slavic regions. A century later, **Ivan the Terrible** set out to expand Russia further. Named the first **tsar**, or emperor, Ivan reformed government, recognized orthodox Christianity, and reorganized the military. However, overextension of resources and his oppressive entourage, the *oprichnina*, depopulated the state and gave him the reputation as a despotic ruler.

Farther south in Central Asia, the Mongol descendants, **Babur** found the **Mughal Empire** of India. Despite his Mongol roots, Babur identified as Turkic due to his tribal origins, and enjoyed support from the powerful Ottoman Empire in Turkey. In 1525, Babur set out for India. By 1529, he had secured land from Kandahar in the west to Bengal in the east; his grandson, **Akbar**, would consolidate the empire, which at the time consisted of small kingdoms. The Mughals would rule India until the eighteenth century and nominally control parts of the country until British takeover in the nineteenth century.

During Mughal rule in India, the Ming dynasty fell in China and the Qing took over. In 1644, the Ming fell to a peasant revolt; the **Manchu**, a non-Han group from the north, took the opportunity to seize Beijing and take the country. Despite their status as non–Han Chinese, the Manchu were accepted; thus began the **Qing dynasty**, under which China would become the dominant power in East Asia and a successful multiethnic state. They would also be China's last imperial rulers, losing power in 1911.

> **DID YOU KNOW?**
>
> The Mughal emperor Shah Jahan built the Taj Mahal in 1631.

Meanwhile, in Persia, the **Safavids** emerged in 1501. A major rival of the Ottoman Empire, the Safavids were a stabilizing force in Asia. Following Sufism, the Safavids supported art, literature, architecture, and other learning. Their organized administration brought order and stability to Persia throughout their rule, which lasted until 1736, when the **Qajar dynasty** took over.

Despite the instability inland, Indian Ocean trade routes had continued to function since at least the seventh century. These oceanic routes connected the Horn of Africa, the East African Coast, the Arabian Peninsula, Southern Persia, India, Southeast Asia, and China. The ocean acted as a unifying force throughout the region, and the **monsoon winds** permitted Arab, Persian, Indian, and Chinese merchants to travel to East Africa in search of goods such as ivory and gold—and slaves.

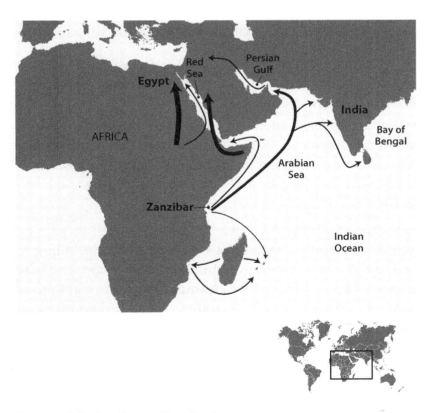

Figure 1.8. Indian Ocean Slave Trade

Despite the civilizational achievements of the Islamic empires, Tang and later Ming dynasty China, and the Central Asian and Indian empires that would emerge from the Mongols, the **East African slave trade** remained vigorous until the nineteenth century. Arabs, Asians, and other Africans kidnapped African people and sent them to lives of slavery throughout the Arab world and South Asia. Later, Europeans would take part in the trade, forcing Africans into slavery in colonies throughout South and Southeast Asia, and on plantations in Indian Ocean islands such as Madagascar.

Further north, the Ottoman Turks represented a threat to Central Europe. Controlling most of Anatolia from the late thirteenth century, the Ottomans spread west into the Balkans, consolidating their rule in 1389 at the **Battle of Kosovo**. In 1453 they captured Istanbul, from which the **Ottoman Empire** would come to rule much of the Mediterranean world.

Under the leadership of **Mehmed the Conqueror** in the fifteenth century and his successors, the Ottomans would conquer Pannonia (Hungary), North Africa, the Caucasus, the Levant and Mesopotamian regions, western Arabia, and Egypt. Under **Suleiman the Magnificent** (1520 – 1566), the **Ottoman Empire** consolidated control over the Balkans, the Middle East, and North Africa and would hold that land until the nineteenth century.

The capture of Istanbul (Constantinople) had represented the true end of the Byzantine Empire; the remaining Christian Byzantines, mainly isolated to coastal Anatolia, Constantinople, and parts of Greece, fled to Italy, bringing Greek, Middle Eastern, and Asian learning with them and enriching the emerging European Renaissance.

THE EUROPEAN RENAISSANCE

The **Renaissance**, or *rebirth*, included the revival of ancient Greek and Roman learning, art, and architecture. Not only did the Renaissance inspire new learning and prosperity in Europe, enabling exploration, colonization, profit, and later imperialism, but it also led to scientific and religious questioning and rebellion against the Catholic Church and, later, monarchical governments.

Reinvigoration of classical knowledge was triggered in part by Byzantine refugees from the Ottoman conquest of Constantinople, including scholars who brought Greek and Roman texts to Italy and Western Europe. The fall of Constantinople precipitated the development of **humanism** in Europe, a mode of thought emphasizing human nature, creativity, and an overarching concept of truth in all philosophical systems (the concept of **syncretism**). Emerging in Italy, the seat of the Catholic Church, humanism was supported by some popes, including Leo X. However in the long term it represented a threat to religious, especially Catholic, orthodoxy, however, as it allowed for the questioning of religious teaching. Ultimately humanism would be at the root of the **Reformation** of the sixteenth century.

Art, considered not just a form of expression but also a science in itself, flourished in fifteenth century Italy, particularly in **Florence**. While artists worked throughout Italy and found patrons in the Vatican among other places, the Florentine **Medici family** funded extensive civic projects, construction, décor, and public sculpture throughout Florence, supporting Renaissance art in that city.

Meanwhile, scholars like Galileo, Isaac Newton, and Copernicus made discoveries in what became known as the **Scientific Revolution**, rooted in the scientific knowledge of the Islamic empires, which had been imported through economic and social contact initiated centuries prior in the Crusades. Scientific study and discovery threatened the power of the Church, whose theological teachings were often at odds with scientific findings and logical reasoning.

> QUICK REVIEW
>
> The Scientific Revolution changed European thinking. What was the impact of using reason and scientific methodology rather than religion to understand the world?

Also in the mid-fifteenth century, in Northern Europe, **Johann Gutenberg** invented the **printing press**; the first book to be published would be the Bible. With the advent of printing, texts could be more widely and rapidly distributed, and people had more access to information beyond what their leaders told them. Combined with humanism and increased emphasis on secular thought, the power of the Church and of monarchs who ruled by divine right was under threat. Here lay the roots of the **Enlightenment**, the basis for reinvigorated European culture and political thought that would drive its development for the next several centuries—and inspire revolution.

Transnational cultural exchange had also resulted in the transmission of technology to Europe. During the sixteenth century, European seafaring knowledge, navigation, and technology benefitted from Islamic and Asian expertise; European explorers and traders could now venture beyond the Mediterranean. Portuguese and Dutch sailors eventually reached India and China, where they established ties with the Ming Dynasty. Trade was no longer dependent on the Silk Road. Improved technology also empowered Europeans to explore overseas, eventually landing in the Western Hemisphere, heretofore unknown to the peoples of Eurasia and Africa.

MESOAMERICAN AND ANDEAN CIVILIZATIONS

In the Americas, the **Maya**, who preceded the Aztecs in Mesoamerica, came to dominate the Yucatán peninsula around 300. They developed a complex spiritual belief system accompanied by relief art, and built pyramidal temples that still stand today. In addition, they developed a detailed calendar and a written language using pictographs similar to Egyptian hieroglyphs; they studied astronomy and mathematics. Maya political administration was organized under monarchical city-states from around 300 until around 900, when the civilization began to decline.

As smaller Mesoamerican civilizations had weakened and collapsed, the **Aztecs** had come to dominate Mexico and much of Mesoamerica. Their military power and militaristic culture allowed the Aztecs to dominate the region and regional trade. The main city of the Aztec empire, **Tenochtitlan**, was founded in 1325 and, at its height, was a major world city home to several million people.

Aztec civilization was militaristic in nature and divided on a class basis: it included slaves, indentured servants, serfs, an independent priestly class, military, and ruling classes. The Aztecs shared many beliefs with the Mayans; throughout Mesoamerica the same calendar was used. Central in the Aztec religion was worship of the god **Quetzalcoatl**, a feathered snake.

Figure 1.9. Quetzalcoatl

Meanwhile, in the Andes, the **Incas** had emerged. Based in **Cuzco**, the Incas had consolidated their power and strengthened in the area, likely due to a surplus of their staple crop maize, around 1300. They were able to conquer local lords and, later, peoples further south, thanks in part to domesticated llamas and alpacas which allowed the military to transport supplies through the mountains.

Inca engineers built the citadel of **Machu Picchu** and imperial infrastructure, including roads throughout the Andes. Thanks to highly developed mountain agriculture, they were able to grow crops at high altitudes and maintain waystations on the highways stocked with supplies.

COLONIZATION OF THE WESTERN HEMISPHERE

Interest in exploration grew in Europe during the Renaissance period. Technological advancements made complex navigation and long-term sea voyages possible, and economic growth resulting from international trade drove interest in market expansion. Global interdependence got a big push from Spain when King Ferdinand and Queen Isabella agreed to sponsor **Christopher Columbus**'s exploratory voyage in 1492 to find a sea route to Asia, in order to speed up commercial trade there. Instead, he stumbled upon the Western Hemisphere, which was unknown to Europeans, Asians, and Africans to this point.

Columbus landed in the Caribbean; he and later explorers would claim the Caribbean islands and eventually Central and South America for Spain and Portugal. However, those areas were already populated by the major American civilizations. Following bloody conflict with the Aztec and Inca Empires, Spain took over the silver- and gold-rich Mesoamerican and Andean territories, and the Caribbean islands where sugar became an important cash crop.

The economic system that resulted was **mercantilism**, whereby the colonizing or *mother country* took raw materials from the territories for the colonizers' own benefit. Governments amassed wealth through protectionism and increasing exports at the expense of other rising colonial powers. This eventually involved developing goods and then selling them back to those colonized lands at an inflated price.

The *encomienda* system granted European landowners the "right" to hold lands in the Americas and demand labor and tribute from the local inhabitants. Spreading Christianity was another important reason for European expansion. Local civilizations and resources were exploited and destroyed.

> QUICK REVIEW
>
> What was destructive about the *encomienda* system?

The **Columbian Exchange** enabled mercantilism to flourish. Conflict and illness brought by the Europeans—especially **smallpox**—decimated the Native Americans, and the Europeans were left without labor to mine the silver and gold or to work the land. **African slavery** was their solution.

Slavery was an ancient institution in many societies worldwide; however, with the Columbian Exchange slavery came to be practiced on a mass scale the likes of which the world had never seen. Throughout Africa and especially on the West African coast, Europeans traded for slaves with some African kingdoms and also raided the land, kidnapping people. European slavers took captured Africans in horrific conditions to the Americas; those who survived were enslaved and forced to work in mining or agriculture for the benefit of expanding European imperial powers.

The Columbian Exchange described the **triangular trade** across the Atlantic: European slavers took kidnapped African people from Africa to the Americas, sold them at auction and exchanged them for sugar and raw materials; these materials were traded in Europe for consumer goods, which were then exchanged in Africa for slaves, and so on.

Enslaved Africans suffered greatly, forced to endure ocean voyages crammed on unsafe, unhygienic ships, sometimes among the dead bodies of other kidnapped people, only to arrive in the Americas to a life of slavery in mines or on plantations. Throughout this period, Africans did resist both on ships and later, in the Americas; **maroon communities** of escaped slaves formed throughout the Western Hemisphere, the **Underground Railroad** in the nineteenth-century United States helped enslaved persons escape the South, and **Toussaint L'Ouverture** led a successful slave rebellion in Haiti, winning independence from the French for that country in 1791.

QUICK REVIEW

Explain the Columbian Exchange.

However, the slave trade continued for centuries. The colonies and later independent countries of the Western Hemisphere continued to practice slavery until the nineteenth century; oppressive legal and social restrictions based on race continue to affect the descendants of slaves to this day throughout the hemisphere.

During the eighteenth century, Spain and Portugal were preeminent powers in global trade thanks to colonization and **imperialism**, the possession and exploitation of land overseas. However, Great Britain became an important presence on the seas; it would later dominate the oceans throughout the nineteenth century.

Though Britain would lose its territories in North America after the American Revolution, it maintained control of the resource-rich West Indies. The kingdom went on to dominate strategic areas in South Africa, New South Wales in Australia, Mauritius in the Indian Ocean, and Madras and Bengal in the Indian Subcontinent, among other places. Later, in the nineteenth century, Britain would expand its empire further. Likewise, France gained territory in North America and in the West Indies; despite losses to Britain in the eighteenth century, that country would also expand its own global empire in the nineteenth century.

SAMPLE QUESTIONS

6) **Which of the following explains why the Eastern Roman Empire remained stable and transitioned to the Byzantine Empire while Rome in Western Europe collapsed?**

   A.   Feudalism contributed to instability in Western Europe, and so that part of the continent disintegrated into a series of small states.

   B.   The schism between the Catholic and Greek Orthodox Churches tore the empire apart.

   C.   Muslims entered Constantinople and took it from Christian Roman control.

   D.   Imprudent alliances in the West led to Roman collapse, while strong leadership and centralization in the East developed a new empire.

Answer:

D.   Correct. Security alliances with Germanic and Gothic tribes left Western Rome vulnerable to their attack; meanwhile in the east, centralized power in Constantinople and strong leadership, particularly under Justinian, led to the rise of the powerful Byzantine Empire.

7)   **Following the death of Muhammad, Muslim leadership became so divided that the religious movement eventually split into Sunnis and Shi'ites. This was due to**

 A.   disagreement over succession to his place as leader.
   B.   disagreement about the importance of conquest.
   C.   disagreement over the theological nature of Islam.
   D.   disagreement over whether to accept Christians and Jews as *People of the Book.*

Answer:

A.   Correct. The Meccan elites believed that they should take over leadership of Islam and continue the movement beyond the Arabian Peninsula; however Ali and Fatima, Muhammad's cousin and daughter, believed Ali was Muhammad's rightful successor as his closest living male relative.

8)   **Despite the violence of the Crusades, they were also beneficial for Europe in that they**

   A.   resulted in substantial, long-term land gains for European leaders in the Middle East.
   B.   introduced European powers to the concept of nation-states, the dominant form of political organization in the Middle East.
 C.   exposed Europe to Islamic and Asian science, technology, and medicine.
   D.   enhanced tolerance of Islam throughout Europe.

Answer:

C.   Correct. Europeans who traveled to the Levant to fight returned home with beneficial knowledge and technology.

9)   **Which of the following was a result of the rise of the Ottoman Turks?**

   A.   Christian Byzantines left Constantinople for Western Europe, bringing classical learning with them.
   B.   The Ottomans were able to conquer the Balkans, the Levant, and eventually North Africa and the Middle East, establishing a large Islamic empire.
   C.   The Ottomans represented an Islamic threat to European Christendom, given their grip on the Balkan Peninsula.
   D.   all of the above

Answer:

D.   Correct. All of the answer choices apply.

10)   **Which of the following best explains the Atlantic Triangular Trade?**

A.   American raw materials were transported to Africa, where they were exchanged for enslaved persons; enslaved persons were taken to the Americas, where they turned raw materials to consumer goods for sale in Europe.

B.   European consumer goods were sold in the Americas at a profit; these goods were also sold in Africa in exchange for raw materials and for enslaved persons, who were taken to the Americas.

C.   European raw materials were sent to the Americas to be transformed into consumer goods by people who had been kidnapped from Africa and enslaved. These consumer goods were then traded in Africa for more slaves.

D.   Enslaved African people were traded in the Americas for raw materials; raw materials harvested by slaves went to Europe where they were utilized and turned to consumer goods; European consumer goods were exchanged in Africa for enslaved people.

Answer:

D.   Correct. American raw materials (like sugar and tobacco) were used in Europe and also turned into consumer goods there. European goods (as well as gold extracted from the Americas) were exchanged in Africa for enslaved persons, who were forced to harvest the raw materials in the Americas.

ARMED CONFLICTS

REFORMATION AND NEW EUROPE

While Spain and Portugal consolidated their hold over territories in the Americas, conflict ensued in Europe. With the cultural changes of the Renaissance, the power of the Catholic Church was threatened; new scientific discoveries and secular Renaissance thought were at odds with many teachings of the Church. The Catholic monk **Martin Luther** wrote a letter of protest to the Pope in 1517 known as the **Ninety-Five Theses**, outlining ways he believed the Church should reform; his ideas gained support, especially among rulers who wanted more power from the Church. Triggering the **Reformation**, or movement for reform of the Church, Luther's ideas led to offshoots of new versions of Christianity in Western Europe, separate from the Orthodox Churches in Russia and Greece. Protestant thinkers like Luther and **John Calvin** addressed particular grievances, condemning the **infallibility** of the Pope (its teaching that the Pope was without fault) and the selling of **indulgences**, or guarantees of entry into heaven.

In Britain, religious and ethnic diversity between Protestant England and Scotland, and Catholic Ireland, made the kingdom unstable. Conflict between Protestants and Catholics was fierce on the Continent as well. The **Thirty Years' War** (1618–1648) began in Central Europe between Protestant nobles in the Holy Roman Empire who disagreed with the strict Catholic **Ferdinand II**, king of Bohemia and eventually archduke of Austria and king of Hungary (what was not under Ottoman domination). Elected Holy Roman Emperor in 1619, Ferdinand II was a leader of the **Counter-Reformation**, attempts at reinforcing Catholic dominance throughout Europe during and after the Reformation in the wake of the Renaissance and related social change. Ferdinand was also closely allied with the Catholic **Hapsburg** Dynasty, which ruled Austria and Spain. Other Protestant-Catholic conflict occurred between Denmark, Sweden, Poland, the Netherlands, and the Papacy.

The tangled alliances between European powers resulted in war between not only France and Spain, but also Sweden and Austria, with the small states of the weakening Holy Roman Empire caught in the middle. The war had been centered on alliances and concerns about the nature of Christianity within different European countries. However, upon signing the 1648 **Treaty of Westphalia**, the European powers agreed to recognize **state sovereignty** and practice **non-interference** in each other's matters—at the expense of family and religious allegiance. 1648 marked a transition into modern international relations when politics and religion would no longer be inexorably intertwined.

The end of the Thirty Years' War represented the end of the notion of the domination of the Catholic Church over Europe and the concept of religious regional dominance, rather than ethnic state divisions. Over the next several centuries, the Church—and religious empires like the Ottomans—would eventually lose control over ethnic groups and their lands, later giving way to smaller **nation-states**.

As state sovereignty became entrenched in European notions of politics, so too did conflict between states. Upon the death of the Hapsburg Holy Roman Emperor **Charles VI** in 1740, the **War of the Austrian Succession** began, a series of Continental wars over who would take over control of the Hapsburg territories. These conflicts would lead to the Seven Years' War.

In 1756 Frederick the Great of Prussia attacked Austria, launching the **Seven Years' War**. In Europe, this war further cemented concepts of state sovereignty and delineated rivalries between European powers engaged in colonial adventure and overseas imperialism—especially Britain and France. It would kick-start British dominance in Asia and also lead to Britain's loss of its North American colonies, nearly bankrupting the Crown.

This time of change in Europe would affect Asia. European concepts of social and political organization became constructed around national sovereignty and nation-states. European economies had become dependent upon colonies and were starting to industrialize, enriching Europe at the expense of its imperial possessions in the Americas, in Africa, and increasingly in Asia.

Industrialization and political organization allowed improved militaries, which put Asian governments at a disadvantage. The major Asian powers—Mughal India, Qing China, the Ottoman Empire, and Safavid (and later, Qajar) Persia—would eventually succumb to European influence or come under direct European control.

THE AGE OF REVOLUTIONS

Monarchies in Europe had been weakened by the conflicts between Catholicism and Protestant faiths; despite European presence and increasing power overseas, as well as its dominance in the Americas, instability made the old order vulnerable. Enlightenment ideals would trigger revolution against **absolute monarchy**. Revolutionary actors drew on the philosophies of enlightenment thinkers like **John Locke**, **Jean-Jacques Rousseau**, and **Montesquieu**, whose beliefs, such as **republicanism**, the **social contract**, the **separation of powers**, and the **rights of man** would drive the Age of Revolutions.

William and Mary defeated James and consolidated Protestant control over England, Scotland, and Ireland under a Protestant constitutional monarchy in the **Glorious Revolution**. The 1689 **English Bill of Rights** established constitutional monarchy, in the spirit of the **Magna Carta**.

The **American Revolution** heavily influenced by Locke, broke out a century later. Please refer to Chapter One, "US History," for details.

The **French Revolution** was the precursor to the end of the feudal order in most of Europe. **King Louis XIV**, the *Sun King* (1643–1715), had consolidated the monarchy in France, taking true political and military power from the nobility. Meanwhile, French Enlightenment thinkers like Jean-Jacques Rousseau, Montesquieu, and **Voltaire** criticized absolute monarchy and the repression of freedom of speech and thought; in 1789, the French Revolution broke out.

The power of the Catholic Church had weakened and the Scientific Revolution and the Enlightenment had fostered social and intellectual change. Colonialism and mercantilism were fueling the growth of an early middle class: people who were not traditionally nobility or landowners under the feudal system were becoming wealthier and more powerful thanks to early capitalism. This class, the **bourgeoisie**, chafed under the rule of the nobility, which had generally inherited land and wealth (while the bourgeoisie earned their wealth in business).

> **DID YOU KNOW?**
>
> Louis XIV built the palace of Versailles to centralize the monarchy—and also to contain and monitor the nobility.

At the same time, panic over dwindling food supplies triggered the **Great Fear** among the enormous population of peasants in July 1789. Suspicion turned to action when the king sent troops to Paris, and on July 14 the people stormed the **Bastille** prison in an event still celebrated in France symbolic of the overthrow of tyranny. Following a period of violence, the monarchy was overthrown.

The French Revolution inspired revolutionary movements throughout Europe and beyond; indeed, the revolutionary principle of self-determination drove revolutionary France to support its ideals abroad.

Ongoing war in Europe and instability in France between republicans and royalists continued to weaken the revolution, but France had military successes in Europe. France had continued its effort to spread the revolution throughout the continent, led by **Napoleon Bonaparte**.

In 1804 Napoleon emerged as emperor of France and proceeded to conquer much of Europe throughout the **Napoleonic Wars**, changing the face of Europe.

By 1815, other European powers had managed to halt France's expansion; at the **Congress of Vienna** in 1815, European powers including Prussia, the Austro-Hungarian Empire, Russia, and Britain agreed on a **balance of power** in Europe. The Congress of Vienna was the first real international peace conference and set the precedent for European political organization.

DID YOU KNOW?

An important tenet of the revolutionary ethos in France was the concept of self-determination, or the right of a people to rule themselves, which threatened rulers fearing revolution in their own countries.

Latin American countries joined Haiti and the United States in revolution against colonial European powers. Inspired by the American and French Revolutions, **Simón Bolivar** led or influenced independence movements in **Venezuela**, **Colombia** (including what is today **Panama**), **Ecuador**, **Peru**, and **Bolivia** in the early part of the nineteenth century.

Figure 1.10. Gran Colombia

EUROPEAN DIVISION

The nineteenth century was a period of change and conflict, and the roots of the major twentieth century conflicts—world war and decolonization—are found in it. Modern European social and political structures and norms, including **nationalism** and the **nation-state**, would begin to emerge. Economic theories based in the Industrial Revolution like **socialism** and eventually **communism** gained traction with the stark class divisions brought on by **urbanization** and industry.

Following the Napoleonic Wars, **Prussia** had come to dominate the German-speaking states that once comprised the Holy Roman Empire. By the nineteenth century and due in part to emphasis on military prowess, Prussia became an important military power and a key ally in the efforts against Napoleon.

Prussia had a particular rivalry with France, having lost several key territories during the Napoleonic Wars. In 1870, the militarily powerful kingdom went to war against France in the **Franco-Prussian War**, during which Prussia took control of **Alsace-Lorraine**, mineral-rich and later essential for industrial development.

Following the Franco-Prussian War, **Otto von Bismarck** unified those linguistically and culturally German states of Central Europe. Prussian power had been growing, fueled by **nationalism** and the **nation-state**, or the idea that individuals with shared experience (including ethnicity, language, religion, and cultural practices) should be unified under one government. In 1871, the **German Empire** became a united state. Bismarck encouraged economic cooperation, instituted army reforms and, perhaps most importantly, created an image of Prussia as a defender of German culture and nationhood, portraying other European states in opposition to that.

The concept of the nation-state spread throughout Central and Eastern Europe, which at the time was controlled by imperial powers like Austria-Hungary and the Ottoman Empire. Nationalism threatened imperial reach. It also led to **Italian Unification**.

IMPERIALISM

As colonialism in the fifteenth and sixteenth centuries had been driven by mercantilism, conquest, and Christian conversion, so was seventeenth, eighteenth and nineteenth century imperialism driven by capitalism, European competition, and conceptions of racial superiority.

Britain and France, historic rivals on the European continent, were also at odds colonizing North America and in overseas trade. During the **Seven Years' War** (1756–1763), considered by many historians to be the first truly global conflict, these two powers fought in Europe and in overseas colonies and interests in North America and Asia.

The **French and Indian War**, as the Seven Years' War is called in North America, resulted in net gains for Britain, which won French colonies in Canada. However, the financial and military strain suffered by Britain in the Seven Years' War made it particularly vulnerable to later rebellion in the Thirteen Colonies, helping the Americans win the Revolutionary War there.

Britain went to war with France in Asia as well. In India, with the decline of the **Mughal Empire** and the rising power of colonial companies specializing in exporting valuable resources like spices and tea, smaller Indian kingdoms were forming alliances with those increasingly influential corporations. By 1803, British interests effectively took control of the Subcontinent and the Mughals were pushed to the north.

Britain would become the strongest naval power in the world and continue to expand its empire, especially in the search for new markets for its manufactured goods to support its industrial economy. During the reign of **Queen Victoria** (1837–1901) the British Empire would expand in Australia, India, and Africa.

Imperial expansion was driven by demand for raw materials for economic growth. The concept of the *white man's burden*, wherein white Europeans were "obligated" to bring their "superior" culture to other civilizations around the globe, also drove imperialist adventure, popularizing it at home in Britain and elsewhere in Europe. Still, other European powers like France, Germany, and even tiny Belgium controlled substantial colonial territory, exploiting natural resources and oppressing the people. Racism was a driving factor in their colonial expansion, too.

> **DID YOU KNOW?**
>
> Major European companies that dominated colonial trade and controlled territory in Asia included the British East India Company, the French East India Company, and the Dutch East India Company.

The European powers were immersed in what became known as the *Scramble for Africa*; the industrial economies of Europe would profit from the natural resources abundant in that continent, and the white man's burden continued to fuel colonization. At the **1884 Berlin Conference**, control over Africa was divided among European powers. Africans were not consulted in this process.

To gain access to closed **Chinese** markets, Britain forced China to buy Indian opium; the **Opium Wars** ended with the **Treaty of Nanking (1842)**. As a consequence, China lost power to Britain and later, other European countries, which gained **spheres of influence**, or areas of China they effectively controlled, and **extraterritoriality**, or privileges in which their citizens were not subject to Chinese law.

> **QUICK REVIEW**
>
> List some of the European powers' justifications for imperialism.

Discontent with the Qing dynasty was growing as Chinese people perceived that their country was coming under control of European imperialists. In 1900, the **Boxer Rebellion**, an uprising led by a Chinese society against the Emperor, was only put down with Western help. Meanwhile, living conditions for Chinese people continued to deteriorate.

In Japan, during the **Meiji Restoration** in 1868, the Emperor Meiji promoted modernization of technology, especially the military. Japan proved itself a world power when it defeated Russia in the **Russo-Japanese War** in 1905, and would play a central role in twentieth century conflict.

INDUSTRIAL REVOLUTION

Throughout this entire period, raw goods fueled European economic growth and development, leading to the **Industrial Revolution** in the nineteenth century. This economic revolution began with textile production in Britain, fueled by cotton from its overseas territories in North America, and later India and Egypt. The first factories were in Manchester, where **urbanization** began as poor people from rural areas flocked to cities in search of higher-paying unskilled jobs in factories.

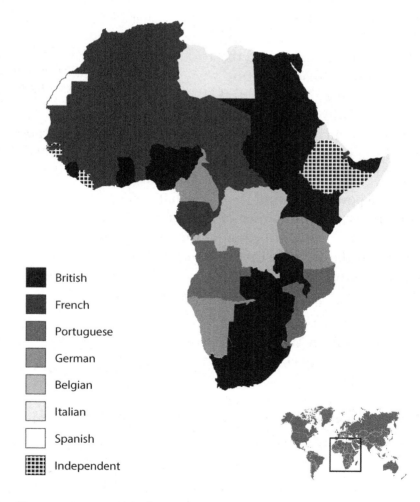

Figure 1.11. Imperial Africa

Early industrial technology sped up the harvesting and transport of crops and their conversion to textiles. This accelerated manufacturing was based on **capitalism**, the *laissez-faire* (or **free market**) theory developed by **Adam Smith**, who believed that an *invisible hand* should guide the marketplace—that government should stay out of the economy regardless of abuses of workers, the environment, or fairness in the marketplace, as the economy would eventually automatically correct for inequalities, price problems, and any other problematic issues.

Technology like the **spinning jenny** and **flying shuttle** exponentially increased the amount of cotton that workers could process into yarn and thread. Iron allowed for stronger machinery and would support the later **Second Industrial Revolution** in the late nineteenth and early twentieth century, which was based on **heavy industry**, railroads, and weapons.

To access the raw materials needed to produce manufactured goods, Britain and other industrializing countries in Western Europe needed resources—hence the drive for imperialism as discussed above. Cotton was harvested in India and Egypt for textile mills, minerals mined in South Africa and the Congo to power metallurgy. Furthermore, as industrialization and urbanization led to the development of early middle classes in Europe and North America, imports of luxury goods like tea, spices, silk, precious metals, and other items from Asia increased to meet consumer demand. Colonial powers also gained by selling manufactured goods back to the colonies from which they had harvested raw materials in the first place, for considerable profit.

Largely unbridled capitalism had led to the conditions of the early Industrial Revolution; workers suffered from abusive treatment, overly long hours, low wages or none at all, and unsafe conditions, including pollution. The German philosophers **Karl Marx** and **Friedrich Engels,** horrified by conditions suffered by industrial workers, developed **socialism**, the philosophy that workers, or the **proletariat,** should own the means of production and reap the profits,

DID YOU KNOW?

The Communist Manifesto contained the famous words *Workers of the world, unite!*

rather than the **bourgeoisie**, who had no interest in the rights of the workers at the expense of profit and who did not experience the same conditions.

A different version of socialism would later help Russia become a major world power. The Russian intellectuals **Vladimir Lenin** and **Leon Trotsky** would take Marx and Engels's theories further, developing **Marxism-Leninism.** They embraced socialist ideals and believed in revolution; however they felt that **communism** could not be maintained under a democratic governing structure. Lenin supported dictatorship, more precisely the *dictatorship of the proletariat*, paving the way for the political and economic organization of the Soviet Union. The Marxist Social Democrats, made up of the **Bolsheviks**, led by **Lenin**, and the **Mensheviks**, would gain power after the fall of the tsar in the early twentieth century. They would eventually take over the country in 1917.

SAMPLE QUESTIONS

11) **The Treaty of Westphalia**

    A.   laid out the final borders of Europe, setting the stage for modern foreign policy.

    B.   established the notion of state sovereignty, in which states recognized each other as independent and agreed not to interfere in each other's affairs.

    C.   gave the Catholic Church more power in the affairs of Catholic-majority countries.

    D.   established the notion of the nation-state, in which culturally and ethnically similar groups would control their own territory as sovereign countries.

Answer:

    B.   **Correct.** The Treaty of Westphalia was based on state sovereignty and non-interference, the core principles of modern international relations.

12) **An important factor leading to the French Revolution was**

    A.   the corruption of Louis XIV.

    B.   the strong organization of the Estates-General.

    C.   support from the United States of America.

    D.   the anti-monarchical philosophies of Enlightenment thinkers like Rousseau and Voltaire.

Answer:

    D.   **Correct.** Enlightenment thinking fueled the Age of Revolutions, and revolutionary French thinkers and writers like Rousseau, Voltaire, and others influenced revolutionary French leaders.

13) **Which of the following is NOT a way that the white man's burden influenced imperialism?**

    A.   It inspired Europeans to settle overseas in order to improve what they believed to be "backward" places.

    B.   Europeans believed in imperialism as in the best interest of native people, who would benefit from adopting European languages and cultural practices.

    C.   Europeans believed it burdensome to be forced to tutor non-Europeans in their languages and customs.

    D.   Many Europeans supported the construction of schools for colonial subjects and even the development of scholarships for them to study in Europe.

Answer:

C.   **Correct.** The idea of the white man's burden was not meant to suggest a literal burden; it was a paternalistic concept of responsibility used to justify imperial dominance.

14)   **Marx and Engels believed**

A.   that the proletariat must control the means of production to ensure a wageless, classless society to meet the needs of all equitably.

B.   in the dictatorship of the proletariat, in which the workers would control the means of production in a non-democratic society.

C.   that an organized revolution directed by a small group of leaders was necessary to bring about social change and a socialist society.

D.   that the bourgeoisie would willingly give up control of the means of production to the proletariat.

Answer:

A.   **Correct.** Marx and Engels believed in abolishing wages and the class structure in exchange for a socialist society where the means of production were commonly held and in which income was equally distributed.

GLOBAL CONFLICTS

WORLD WAR I

Instability in the Balkans and increasing tensions in Europe culminated with the assassination of the Austro-Hungarian Archduke **Franz Ferdinand** by the Serbian nationalist **Gavrilo Princip** in Sarajevo on June 28, 1914. In protest of continuing Austro-Hungarian control over Serbia, Princip's action kicked off the **system of alliances** that had been in place among European powers.

Austria-Hungary declared war on Serbia, and Russia came to Serbia's aid. As an ally of Austria-Hungary, Germany declared war on Russia. Russia's ally France prepared for war; as Germany traversed Belgium to invade France, Belgium pleaded for aid from other European countries and so Britain declared war on Germany.

Germany had been emphasizing military growth since the consolidation and militarization of the empire under Bismarck in the mid-nineteenth century. Now, under **Kaiser Wilhelm II**, who sought expanded territories in Europe and overseas for Germany (including the potential capture of overseas British and French colonies), Germany was a militarized state and an important European power in its own right.

> **DID YOU KNOW?**
>
> The first international war to use industrialized weaponry, WWI was called "the Great War" because battle on such a scale had never before been seen.

In Europe, the 1914 **Battle of the Marne** between Germany and French and British forces defending France resulted in trench warfare that would continue for years, marking the Western Front. At **Gallipoli** in 1915, Australian and New Zealander troops fought the **Ottoman Empire**, allies of Germany, near Istanbul. Later that year, a German submarine, or **U-boat**, sank the *Lusitania*, a passenger ship in the Atlantic, killing many American civilians. In 1916, the **Battle of Verdun**, the longest battle of the war, ended in the failure of the Germans to defeat the French army. In 1916, the British navy pushed back the German navy in the **Battle of Jutland**; despite heavy losses, Britain was able to ensure that German naval power was diminished for the rest of the war. On July 1, 1916, the **Battle of the Somme** became part of an allied effort to repel Germany using artillery to end the stalemate on the Western Front; after four months, however, the front moved only five miles.

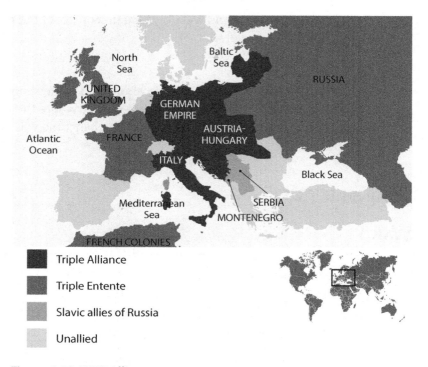

Figure 1.12. WWI Alliances

Finally, in 1917, the United States caught the **Zimmerman Telegram**, in which Germany secretly proposed an alliance with Mexico to attack the US. This finally spurred US intervention in the war; despite Russian withdrawal after the Bolshevik Revolution in October 1917, Germany was forced to surrender in the face of invasion by the US-supported allies.

According to the **Schlieffen Plan**, Germany had planned to fight a war on two fronts against both Russia and France. However, Russia's unexpectedly rapid mobilization stretched the German army too thin on the Eastern Front, while it became bogged down in **trench warfare** on the Western Front against the British, French, and later the Americans. Germany lost the war and was punished with the harsh **Treaty of Versailles,** which held it accountable for the entirety of the war. The Treaty brought economic hardship on the country by forcing it to pay **reparations**. Wilhelm was forced to abdicate and never again regained power in Germany. German military failure and consequent economic collapse due to the Treaty of Versailles and later worldwide economic depression set the stage for the rise of fascism and Adolf Hitler.

The Treaty also created the **League of Nations**, an international organization designed to prevent future outbreaks of international war; however, it was largely toothless, especially because the powerful United States did not join.

CHANGE IN THE MIDDLE EAST

The end of WWI also marked the end of the Ottoman Empire, which was officially dissolved in 1923. At the end of the war the Middle East was divided into **mandates**. The borders were decided by the **Sykes-Picot Agreement** between Britain and France, which divided the region into spheres of influence to be controlled by each power, and are essentially those national borders that divide the Middle East today.

In 1917, the secret **Balfour Declaration** promised the Jews an independent state in Palestine, but Western powers did not honor this agreement. In fact it conflicted directly with the Sykes-Picot Agreement, which held that Palestine would be governed internationally. The state of Israel was not established until 1948.

After the First World War, the secular nationalist **Mustafa Ataturk**, one of the Young Turks who pushed a secular, nationalist agenda, kept European powers out of Anatolia and abolished the Caliphate in 1924, establishing modern Turkey.

There was no more Caliph. Refugees and migrants had traveled throughout the Ottoman Empire over the course of the war, suddenly restricted by international borders from their places of origin. People lacked identification papers. Ethnic and religious groups were divided by what would become the borders of the modern Middle East.

The roots of two competing ideologies, **Pan-Arabism** and **Islamism**, developed in this context. According to Pan-Arabism, Arabs and Arabic speakers should be aligned regardless of international borders. Pan-Arabism eventually became an international movement espousing Arab unity in response to European and US influence and presence later in the twentieth century.

Islamism began as a social and political movement. The **Muslim Brotherhood** was established in Egypt in the 1920s, filling social roles that the state had abandoned or could not fill.

> **DID YOU KNOW?**
>
> In 1915, the Ottoman Empire launched a genocide against the Christian Armenian people, part of a campaign to control ethnic groups it believed threatened the Turkish nature of the empire. An estimated 1.5 million Armenians were forcibly removed from their homes and killed. To this day, the Turkish government denies the Armenian Genocide.

Eventually taking a political role, the Muslim Brotherhood's model later inspired groups like Hamas and Hezbollah.

RUSSIAN REVOLUTION

By 1917, Russia was suffering from widespread food shortages and economic crisis; morale was low due to conscription and as the military suffered enormous losses and humiliating defeats under the command of Nicholas II. During WWI, this combination of failures at home and on the front only added to widespread dissatisfaction with the rule of the Tsar. The Tsar was forced to abdicate, and a period of violence and instability followed as different factions fought for power.

The communist Bolsheviks, led by Lenin and Trotsky, consolidated their power by nationalizing industry, developing and distributing propaganda portraying themselves as the defenders of Russia against imperialism, and forcefully eliminating dissent. Yet for many, it was more appealing to fight for a new Russia with hope for an improved standard of living than to return to the old times under the Tsar. In the **October Revolution** Lenin, Trotsky, and the Bolsheviks took control of Russia. By 1921, the Bolsheviks were victorious and formed the **Soviet Union** or **Union of Soviet Socialist Republics (USSR)**.

> **DID YOU KNOW?**
>
> In the 1920s, around twenty million Russians were sent to the *gulags*, or prison labor camps, usually in Siberia, thousands of miles from their homes. Millions died.

Following Lenin's death in 1924, the Secretary of the Communist Party, **Josef Stalin**, took power. Under Stalin's totalitarian dictatorship, the USSR became socially and politically repressive; the Communist Party and the military underwent **purges** where any persons who were a potential threat to Stalin's power were imprisoned or executed.

In 1931, Stalin enforced the **collectivization** of land and agriculture in an attempt to consolidate control over the countryside and improve food security. He had the *kulaks*, or landowning peasants, sent to the *gulags*, enabling the government to confiscate their land. By 1939, most farming and land was controlled by the government, and most peasants lived on collective land. However, systemic disorganization in the 1920s and 1930s resulted in famine and food shortages.

Stalin also focused on accelerating industrial development. Targeting heavy industry, these **Five Year Plans** increased production in industrial materials and staples like electricity, petroleum, coal, and iron; they also resulted in the construction of major infrastructure throughout the country from 1929–1938. However, conditions for the workers were dismal. The USSR quickly became an industrial power, but at the expense of millions who lost their lives in purges, forced labor camps, and famine.

CHANGE IN EAST ASIA

Following its victory in the Russo-Japanese War, Japan was recognized as a military power. It joined a world focused on industry and imperialism.

Having already embraced industrialization and modern militarization, Japan turned towards imperialism throughout Asia. In the **First Sino-Japanese War** (1894–1895), Japan gained influence and territory in mainland Asia. This conflict also revealed Chinese military and organizational limitations and showed Japanese military superiority.

Following the First World War, despite having provided assistance to the French and British in Asia, Japan began its own imperialist adventure in East and Southeast Asia not only to gain power and access to raw materials, but also to limit and eventually expel European rule in what Japan considered its *sphere of influence*. In 1931, Japan invaded **Manchuria**, creating the puppet state *Manchukuo*.

Meanwhile, China was undergoing political change. The **Xinhai Revolution** broke out in 1911, resulting in the overthrow of the Qing and the end of dynastic Chinese rule. However, despite Republican recognition by major international powers, the power vacuum left by the end of imperial China allowed the rise of warlords throughout the enormous country, and the government was unable to establish total control.

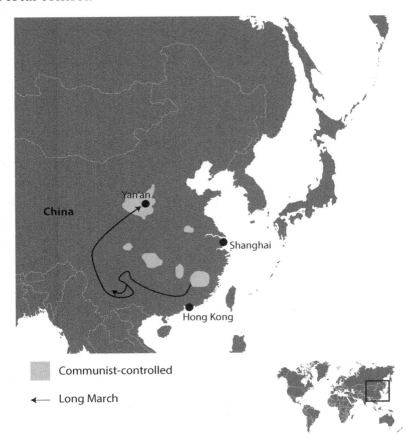

Figure 1.13. The Long March

The **Kuomintang (KMT)**, or Nationalist Party of the revolutionary government worked to consolidate government power; the KMT leader **Chiang Kai-shek** (or **Jiang Jieshi**) went on to take control of much of China back from the warlords.

At the same time, communism was emerging in China as a response to western imperialism. Temporarily working together, the KMT and **Chinese Communist Party** CCP were able to bring Chinese territory back under Republican control. However, Chiang turned against the CCP in 1927, driving it south.

The CCP focused its organizing activities in the countryside on the peasants, becoming powerful in southern China. Ongoing KMT attacks forced the CCP to retreat on the **Long March** north. During this time of hardship, **Mao Zedong** emerged as the leader of the movement.

World War II

Meanwhile, Germany suffered under the provisions of the Treaty of Versailles. In 1919, a democratic government was established at Weimar—the **Weimar Republic**. Germany was in chaos; the Kaiser had fled and the country was torn apart by war. However, the new government could not bring stability.

Blamed for WWI, Germany owed huge **reparations** according to the treaty to pay for the cost of the war, setting off **hyperinflation** and impoverishing the country and its people. The rise of communists and a workers' party that came to be known as the National Socialist Party, or **Nazi Party**, led to further political instability. Following the crash of the stock market in 1929, German unemployment reached six million; furthermore, the United States had called in its foreign loans. The Nazis, led by **Adolf Hitler**, gained support from business interests, which feared communist power in government.

Hitler maneuvered into the role of chancellor by 1933. His charisma and popular platform—to cancel the Treaty of Versailles—allowed him to rise. Nazi ideals appealed strongly to both industry and the workers in the face of global economic depression. Moreover, the Nazi Minister of Propaganda **Joseph Goebbels** executed an effective propaganda campaign, and would do so throughout Hitler's rule, known as the **Third Reich**.

Taking advantage of a series of crises, Hitler became the undemocratic *Führer*, or *leader*, of Germany, and the Nazis consolidated total control. They also set into motion their agenda of racism and genocide against "non-Aryan" (non-Germanic) or "racially impure" people.

Jewish people were particularly targeted. Germany had a considerable Jewish population; so did the other Central and Eastern European countries that Germany would come to control. Throughout the 1930s, the Nazis passed a series of laws limiting Jewish rights. **Kristallnacht** took place in 1938, an organized series of attacks on Jewish businesses, homes, and places of worship.

In 1939, Jews were forced from their homes into **ghettoes**, isolated and over-crowded urban neighborhoods. Millions of Jewish people were sent to **concentration camps**; the Nazis decided on the **Final Solution** to the "Jewish Question": to murder Jewish people by systematically gassing them at death camps. At least six million European Jews were murdered by the Nazis in the **Holocaust**.

Roma, Slavic people, homosexuals, disabled people, people of color, prisoners of war, communists, and others were also forced into slave labor in concentration camps and murdered there. Later, this concept of torturing and killing people based on their ethnicity in order to exterminate them would become defined as **genocide**.

Hitler was a **fascist**, believing in a mostly free market accompanied by a dictatorial government with a strong military. He sought to restore Germany's power and expand its reach through annexation and conquest. In 1939 Germany invaded **Poland** in what is commonly considered the beginning of the **Second World War**.

> **DID YOU KNOW?**
>
> The Atlantic Charter described values shared by the US and Britain, including restoring self-governance in occupied Europe and liberalizing international trade.

War exploded in Europe in 1939. Hitler gained control of more land than any European power since Napoleon, undefeated until the **Battle of Britain**. Despite staying out of combat, in 1941 the United States provided support and military aid to Britain through the **Lend-Lease Act**.

When Japan joined the **Axis** powers of Germany and Italy, the **Chinese Civil War** between communists and nationalists was interrupted by the Second Sino-Japanese War, when Japan tried to extend its imperial reach deeper into China.

At this time, Chiang was forced to form an alliance with Mao and the two forces worked together against Japan. By the end of the war, the CCP was stronger than ever, with widespread support from many sectors of Chinese society, while the KMT was demoralized and had little popular support.

In December of 1941, Japan, now part of the **Axis** along with Germany and Italy, attacked the United States at Pearl Harbor. Consequently, the US joined the war in Europe and in the Pacific, deploying thousands of troops in both theaters. Meanwhile, Japan continued its imperialist policies throughout Asia, threatening European interests and colonies there.

Back in Europe, having broken a promise to the Soviet Union, Hitler invaded Russia. But in 1942, the USSR defeated Germany at the **Battle of Stalingrad**, a turning point in the war during which the Nazis were forced to turn from the Eastern Front.

In 1944, the Allies invaded France on **D-Day**. While they liberated Paris in August, the costly **Battle of the Bulge** extended into 1945. Despite thousands of American casualties, Hitler's forces were pushed back. In the spring of 1945, when American and Soviet forces entered Germany, the Allies accepted Germany's surrender.

The war in the Pacific would continue, however. An American invasion of Japan would have likely resulted in hundreds of thousands of casualties. To avoid this, 1945, the US bombed the Japanese cities of **Hiroshima** and **Nagasaki** with nuclear weapons in 1945, the only time they have been used in combat. The tremendous civilian casualties did force the Emperor to surrender; at that point, the Second World War came to an end.

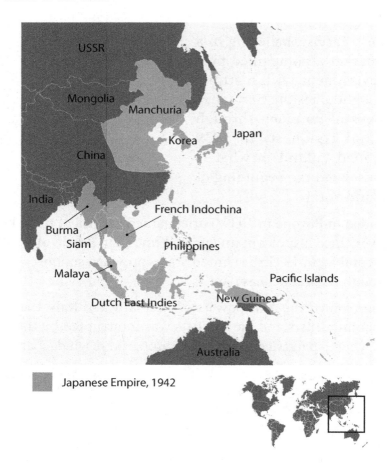

Figure 1.14. Japanese Expansion in Asia

That year in China, the Chinese Civil War recommenced; by 1949 the communists had emerged victorious. The KMT withdrew to Taiwan, while Mao and the CCP took over China, which became a communist country.

The extreme horrors of WWII helped develop the concept of **genocide**, or the effort to extinguish an entire group of people because of their ethnicity, and the idea of **human rights**. The **United Nations** was formed, based on the League of Nations, as a body to champion human rights and uphold international security. Its **Security Council** is made up of permanent member states which can intervene militarily in the interests of international stability.

Allied forces took the lead in rebuilding efforts: the US occupied areas in East Asia and Germany, while the Soviet Union remained in Eastern Europe. The Allies had planned to rebuild Europe according to the **Marshall Plan**; however, the USSR occupied eastern European countries, and they came under communist control. The **Cold War** had begun.

THE COLD WAR

At the Yalta Conference in February 1945, Stalin, Churchill, and Roosevelt had agreed upon the division of Germany, the free nature of government in Poland, and free elections in Eastern Europe. However, at the **Potsdam Conference** in July 1945, things had changed. Harry Truman had replaced Franklin D. Roosevelt, who had died in office, and Clement Atlee had replaced Winston Churchill. Stalin felt betrayed by the US use of the atomic bomb; likewise, the US and the British felt that Stalin had violated the agreement at Yalta regarding democracy in Eastern Europe.

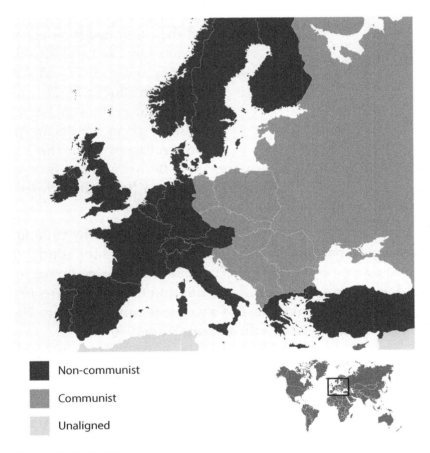

Figure 1.15. Cold War Europe

Stalin ensured that communists came to power in Eastern Europe, setting up satellite states at the Soviet perimeter in violation of the Yalta agreement. The Soviet rationale was to establish a buffer zone following its extraordinarily heavy casualties in WWII—around twenty million. In the words of the British Prime Minister

Winston Churchill, an *iron curtain* had come down across Europe, dividing east from west.

Consequently, western states organized the North Atlantic Treaty Organization or **NATO,** an agreement wherein an attack on one was an attack on all; this treaty provided for **collective security** in the face of the Soviet expansionist threat. The United States adopted a policy of **containment,** the idea that communism should be *contained,* as part of the **Truman Doctrine** of foreign policy.

In response, the Soviet Union created the **Warsaw Pact,** a similar organization consisting of Eastern European communist countries. **Nuclear weapons** raised the stakes of the conflict. The concept of **mutually-assured destruction,** or the understanding that a nuclear strike by one country would result in a response by the other, ultimately destroying the entire world, may have prevented the outbreak of active violence.

Germany itself had been divided into four zones, controlled by Britain, France, the US, and the USSR. Berlin had been divided the same way. Once Britain, France, and the US united their zones into West Germany in 1948 and introduced a new currency, the USSR cut off West Berlin in the **Berlin Blockade.** For nearly a year western powers provided supplies to West Berlin by air in the **Berlin Airlift.** Until 1961, refugees from the Eastern Bloc escaped to West Berlin. Furthermore, West Berlin was a center for Western espionage. In 1961, the USSR, now led by **Nikita Khrushchev,** closed the border and constructed the **Berlin Wall.**

QUICK REVIEW

How did the Cold War erupt between the Allies and the Soviet Union?

Korea had also been divided after the war, controlled by communists north of the **thirty-eighth parallel.** In 1950, the north invaded the south with Russian and Chinese support. According to the Truman Doctrine, communism needed to be contained. Furthermore, according to **domino theory,** if one country became communist, then more would, too, like a row of dominoes falling. Therefore, the United States became involved in the **Korean War** (1950 – 1953).

UN troops led by the US came to the aid of the South Koreans; China supported the North Koreans. War on the peninsula ended in a stalemate in 1953; tensions continue today.

Later, in **Cuba,** the revolutionary **Fidel Castro** took over in 1959. Allied with the Soviet Union, he allowed missile bases to be constructed in Cuba, which threatened the United States. During the **Cuban Missile Crisis** in 1962, the world came closer than ever to nuclear war when the USSR sent missiles to Cuba. President Kennedy and Premier Khrushchev were able to come to an agreement, and nuclear war was averted.

Despite this success, the United States engaged in a lengthy violent conflict in Southeast Asia. Supporting anti-communist fighters in Vietnam in keeping with containment and domino theory, the United States pursued the **Vietnam War** for almost a decade. The communist **Viet Cong** were waging a guerrilla war against France for independence, and the US became involved in the 1960s when France asked for aid.

Despite being outnumbered, Viet Cong familiarity with the difficult terrain, support from Russia and China, and determination eventually resulted in victory. Bloody guerrilla warfare demoralized the American military, but the 1968 **Tet Offensive** was a turning point. Despite enormous losses, the North Vietnamese won a strategic victory in this coordinated, surprise offensive. Extreme objection to the war within the United States, high casualties, and demoralization eventually resulted in US withdrawal in 1973.

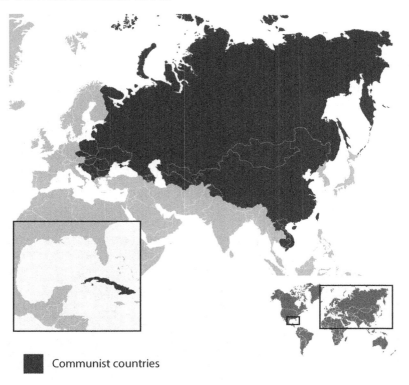

Communist countries

Figure 1.16. The Communist World

Toward the end of the 1960s and into the 1970s, the Cold War reached a period of **détente**, or a warming of relations. The US and USSR entered into arms treaties like the **Nuclear Non-Proliferation Treaty** and the **Strategic Arms Limitation Treaty** (**SALT I**). Some cultural exchanges and partnerships in outer space took place.

At the same time, the United States began making diplomatic overtures toward communist China. China and the USSR had difficult relations due to their differing views on the nature of

DID YOU KNOW?

Perhaps the most famous proposal in weapons technology of the Cold War was the Strategic Defense Initiative; popularly known as *Star Wars*, this outer-space based system would have intercepted Soviet intercontinental ballistic missiles.

communism. Following the **Sino-Soviet Split** of the 1960s, China had lost much Soviet support for its modernization programs. Despite advances in agriculture and some industrialization, Mao's programs like the **Great Leap Forward** had harmed the people. In 1972, US President Richard Nixon visited China, establishing relations between the communist government and the United States. Communist China joined the UN.

The climate would change again, however, in the 1970s and 1980s. The US and USSR engaged in proxy wars worldwide. In addition, the **arms race** was underway. President Ronald Reagan focused on weapons development in order to outspend the USSR on military technology.

DECOLONIZATION

Meanwhile, the former colonies of the fallen European colonial powers had won or were in the process of gaining their independence.

In 1949, the Indian leader **Mohandas Gandhi** had led a peaceful independence movement against the British, winning Indian independence. His assassination by Hindu radicals led to conflict between Hindus and Muslims in the **Subcontinent**, resulting in **Partition,** the bloody division of India into Pakistan and eventually Bangladesh.

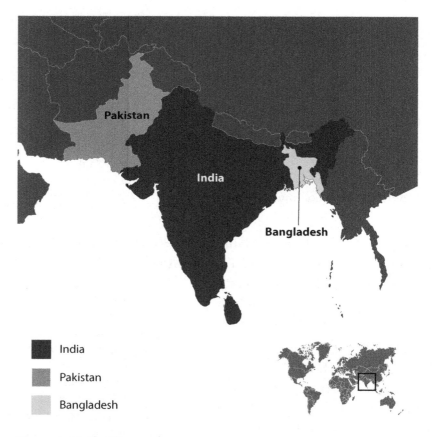

Figure 1.17. Partition

Bloody conflict in Africa like the **Algerian War** against France (1954–1962), the **Mau Mau Rebellion** against the British in Kenya in the 1950s, and violent movements against Belgium in the **Congo** resulted in African independence for many countries in the 1950s, 1960s, and 1970s; likewise, so did strong leadership by African nationalist leaders and thinkers like **Jomo Kenyatta**, **Julius Nyerere**, and **Kwame Nkrumah.** The apartheid regime in South Africa, where segregation between races was legal and people of color lived in oppressive conditions, was not lifted until the 1990s; **Nelson Mandela** led the country in a peaceful transition process.

In the Middle East, the European-controlled protectorates became independent states with arbitrary borders drawn and rulers installed by the Europeans. The creation of the state of **Israel** was especially contentious: in the 1917 **Balfour Declaration**, the British had promised the **Zionist** movement of European Jews a homeland; however, the US assured the Arabs in 1945 that a Jewish state would not be founded there. Israel emerged from confusion, chaos, and tragedy after the Holocaust in Europe, and violence on the ground in Palestine carried out by both Jews and Arabs. The conflict continues in the region today.

> **DID YOU KNOW?**
>
> The revolutionary Iranian government would go on to support Shi'a militants (the *Hezbollah,* or the *Party of God*) in the **Lebanese Civil War** throughout the 1980s; this group is also inspired by Islamism.

In Egypt, **Gamal Abdul Nasser** led the Pan-Arabist movement in the region. Egypt led the unsuccessful **Six Day War** in 1967 against Israel, a major setback for the Arab states. Israel took control of Arab territory. The Arab-Israeli conflict became a Cold War conflict during the 1973 **Yom Kippur War**: the US supported **Israel** and the USSR supported **Syria** and **Egypt**. Conflict continued until 1978, when the American president Jimmy Carter brokered peace between Israel and Egypt (and later, Jordan) in the **Camp David Accords**. By the 1970s, Pan-Arabism was no longer the popular, unifying movement it had once been.

The **Non-Aligned Movement** arose in response to the Cold War. Instead of the bipolar world of the Cold War (one democratic, led by the US, the other communist, led by the USSR), the Non-Aligned Movement sought an alternative: the **Third World**. Non-Aligned or Third World countries wanted to avoid succumbing to the influence of either of the superpowers, and many found a forum in the United Nations in which to strengthen their international profiles.

However, throughout the Cold War, **proxy wars** between the US and the USSR were fought around the world. In the 1980s, the United States began supporting anti-communists in Nicaragua, Afghanistan, Angola, Mozambique, and Ethiopia.

Iran had been under the oppressive regime of the western-supported **Shah Reza Pahlavi** for decades. By the 1970s, the Shah's corrupt, oppressive regime

> **QUICK REVIEW**
>
> Why were proxy wars important in the context of the Cold War?

was extremely unpopular in Iran, but it was propped up by the West. In the 1979 **Iranian Revolution**, diverse forces overthrew the Shah; shortly afterward, Islamist revolutionaries took over the country and established a conservative theocracy led by **Ayatollah Khomeini**.

Following the Iranian Revolution, the Iraqi leader **Saddam Hussein** declared war against Iran. While governed by Sunnis, Iraq was actually a Shi'ite-majority country, and Saddam feared Iran would trigger a similar revolution there. Iraq also sought control over strategic and oil-rich territories. The war raged from 1980 – 1990.

SAMPLE QUESTIONS

15) **Which of the following was a weakness of the Schlieffen Plan?**

A.   It overstretched the German army.

B.   It failed to anticipate a stronger resistance in France.

C.   It underestimated Russia's ability to mobilize its troops.

D.   all of the above

Answer:

D.   Correct. All of the answer choices are true.

16) **According to the Sykes-Picot Agreement,**

A.   Israel would become an independent state.

B.   Husayn ibn Ali would become Caliph.

C.   Ataturk would lead an independent Turkey.

D.   Palestine would be under international supervision.

Answer:

D.   Correct. Sykes-Picot put Palestine under the supervision of various international powers.

17) **Which of the following led to the rise of the Nazis in early 1930s Germany?**

A.   the impact of reparations and the support of German industrialists

B.   the impact of the Great Depression and the support of the workers

C.   support from the international communist movement and the impact of reparations on the German economy

D.   support from German industrialists and strong backing from other political factions in the Reichstag

Answer:

A.   Correct. The Nazis planned to cease paying reparations, so their nationalist approach appealed to many Germans suffering from the hyperinflation that reparations had triggered. Furthermore, the

Nazis had the support of German industrialists, who feared the rise of communism among the working classes.

18) **The Cold War was rooted in**

A.   Stalin's unwillingness to cede control of East Berlin to the allies following the fall of the Nazis.

B.   the erection of the Berlin Wall.

C.   Stalin's failure to honor the agreement at Yalta, installing communist regimes in Eastern Europe rather than permitting free, democratic elections.

D.   the Cuban Missile Crisis.

Answer:

C.   Correct. The Cold War was rooted in Stalin's creation of communist satellite states in Eastern and Central Europe.

19) **Which of the following precipitated the end of the Cold War?**

A.   the Iran Hostage Crisis

B.   the Soviet War in Afghanistan

C.   the Iran-Iraq War

D.   the Yom Kippur War

Answer:

B.   Correct. The Soviet invasion of Afghanistan and the subsequent ten-year war sapped Soviet financial and military resources—and morale. This draining war, plus the high price of the arms race with the United States, contributed significantly to the fall of the Soviet Union.

POST–COLD WAR WORLD

In 1991, the Soviet Union fell when Soviet Premier **Mikhail Gorbachev**, who had implemented reforms like *glasnost* and *perestroika* (or *openness* and *transparency*), was nearly overthrown in a coup; a movement led by **Boris Yeltsin**, who had been elected president of Russia, stopped the coup. The USSR was dissolved later that year and Yeltsin became president of the Russian Federation. War in Afghanistan and military overspending in an effort to keep up with American military spending had weakened the USSR to the point of collapse, and the Cold War ended.

COLD WAR CONSEQUENCES

In 1990, Saddam Hussein, the leader of Iraq, invaded Kuwait, threatening the global oil supply. In response, the United States and other countries went to war—with a

UN mandate—to regain control of the world's petroleum reserves. The **Gulf War** cemented the US status as the sole superpower.

The changes following the fall of the Iron Curtain led to instability in the Balkans. In 1992, Bosnia declared its independence from the collapsing state of Yugoslavia. Violence broke out, and the **Bosnian War** raged from 1992 to 1995, resulting another European genocide—this time, of Bosnian Muslims.

Also following the Cold War, proxy wars throughout the world and instability in former colonies continued. In 1994, conflict in Central Africa resulted in the **Rwandan Genocide**. In **Zaire**, the country descended into instability following the fall of **Mobutu Sese Seko**, the US-supported dictator, in 1997.

In the 1980s, drought in the Horn of Africa led to widespread famine. The general public became more concerned about providing foreign aid to the suffering. In 1991 **Somalia** was broken up under the control of various warlords and clans; civilians suffered from starvation and violence even after a failed military intervention led by the United States. To this day there is no central government in much of Somalia.

COOPERATION AND CONFLICT

Following the end of the Cold War and post-decolonization, the balance of economic and political power began to change. The **G-20**, the world's twenty most important economic and political powers, includes many former colonies and non-European countries. The **BRICS**—Brazil, Russia, India, China, and South Africa—are recognized as world economic and political leaders.

Steps toward European unification had begun as early as the 1950s; the **European Union**, as it is known today, was formed in 1992. As the former Soviet satellite states moved from communism to more democratic societies and capitalistic economies, more countries partnered with the EU and eventually joined it, with twenty-eight members in 2015 and more in negotiations to join. However, European populism and rejection of globalism is rising: the United Kingdom voted to withdraw from the EU in 2016.

European Union countries remain independent, but they cooperate in international affairs, justice, security and foreign policy, environmental matters, and economic policy. Many also share a common currency, the **euro**.

Continental integration exists beyond Europe. In Africa, the **African Union** is a forum for African countries to organize and align political, military, economic, and other policies. It also organizes peacekeeping missions.

Globalization opened international markets through free-trade agreements like **NAFTA** (the North American Free Trade Agreement) and **Mercosur** (the South American free-trade zone). The **World Trade Organization** oversees international trade. Technological advances like improvements in transportation infrastructure and the **internet** made international communication faster, easier and cheaper.

However, more open borders, reliable international transportation, and faster, easier worldwide communication brought risks, too. The United States was attacked by terrorists on **September 11, 2001**, resulting in thousands of civilian casualties.

Following the attacks on 9/11, the United States attacked Afghanistan as part of the **War on Terror**. Afghanistan's radical Islamist **Taliban** government was providing shelter to the group that took responsibility for the attacks, **al Qaeda**. Led by **Osama bin Laden**, al Qaeda was inspired by Islamism and also by the radical Wahhabism of the Saudis. Bin Laden was killed by the United States in 2011 and control of Afghan security was turned over to the Afghan government in 2014, but the US still maintains a strong military presence in the country.

> **DID YOU KNOW?**
>
> While benefits of international trade include lower prices and more consumer choice, unemployment often increases in more developed countries, and labor and environmental violations are more likely in developing countries.

The Iraq War began in 2003 when the US invaded that country under the faulty premise that Saddam Hussein's regime was involved with al Qaeda and possessed weapons of mass destruction intended for terrorism. The war resulted in thousands of civilian and military casualties, destabilizing the region.

Elsewhere in the Middle East, reform movements began via the 2011 **Arab Spring**. Some dictatorial regimes have been replaced with democratic governments; other countries still experience limited freedoms or even civil unrest. In Syria, unrest erupted into an ongoing civil war. One consequence has been enormous movements of refugees into Europe, a factor in some Europeans' rejection of globalism.

Today, the Islamic State of Iraq and al Sham (**ISIS**) referring to Iraq and Syria (or Islamic State of Iraq and the Levant—ISIL) has arisen. ISIS has established a de facto state in Iraq and Syria with extremist Islamist policies and presents a global terror threat.

SAMPLE QUESTIONS

20) **While immediately after the fall of the Soviet Union the US emerged as the sole superpower, in the twenty-first century, which phenomenon has so far characterized global governance?**

　　A.　international terrorism

　　B.　international economic and political organizations

　　C.　international conflict

　　D.　the European Union

Answer:

　　B.　**Correct.** While the United States remains a leading world power, the emergence of international organizations like the BRICS, the EU, the G-20, and the AU has empowered other countries; furthermore, international trade agreements are helping mold the international balance of power.

21) **What was one reason for the Bosnian War?**

A.   attacks by Bosniak Islamic extremists

B.   the dissolution of Yugoslavia

C.   the separation of Yugoslavia from the USSR

D.   attacks by Middle Eastern Islamic extremists

Answer:

B.   Correct. One reason for the Bosnian War was the Yugoslav government's attempt to force the country to stay together; following the end of the Cold War and the collapse of communism, the formerly communist Yugoslavia had started to break up.

22) **What is one major role that the African Union plays?**

A.   The AU is a free trade area.

B.   The AU manages a single currency.

C.   The AU manages several peacekeeping forces.

D.   The AU represents individual African countries in international diplomacy.

Answer:

C.   Correct. The AU organizes and manages peacekeeping forces in Africa; it also cooperates with the United Nations in peacekeeping.

23) **Which of the following is NOT a reason that the Soviet Union collapsed?**

A.   glasnost

B.   perestroika

C.   the war in Afghanistan

D.   the rise of the Taliban

Answer:

D.   Correct. The Taliban did not emerge in Afghanistan until well after Soviet withdrawal from the country.

24) **Despite his alliance with the US-supported *mujahideen* in the war in Afghanistan against the Soviets, Osama bin Laden sponsored attacks against the United States because**

A.   he opposed a US military presence in Saudi Arabia.

B.   he opposed US support of Israel.

C.   he wanted to establish a global Islamist regime in accordance with the extremist, unorthodox beliefs rooted in Wahhabism.

D.   all of the above

Answer:

D.   Correct. Bin Laden cited all of these reasons for his violent acts.

2

US History

NORTH AMERICA BEFORE EUROPEAN CONTACT

NORTHEASTERN SOCIETIES

Prior to European colonization, diverse Native American societies controlled the continent; they would later come into economic and diplomatic contact, and military conflict, with European colonizers and United States forces and settlers.

Major civilizations that would play an important and ongoing role in North American history included the **Iroquois** and **Algonquin** in the Northeast. Both of those tribes would also be important allies of the English and French, respectively, in future conflicts, in that part of the continent.

The Iroquois actually consisted of five tribes, the **Mohawk, Seneca, Cayuga, Oneida,** and **Onondaga**—which organized into the regionally powerful **Iroquois Confederacy**, bringing stability to the eastern Great Lakes region.

While many Native American, or First Nations, people speak variants of the Algonquin language, the **Algonquin** people themselves have historically been a majority in what is today Quebec and the Great Lakes region. Active in the fur trade, the Algonquin developed important relationships with French colonizers and a rivalry with the Iroquois.

THE MIDWEST

Later, the young United States would come into conflict with the Shawnee, Lenape, Kickapoo, Miami, and other tribes in the Midwestern region of Ohio, Illinois, Indiana, and Michigan in early western expansion. These tribes later formed the **Northwest Confederacy** to fight the United States.

The **Shawnee** were an Algonquin-speaking people based in the Ohio Valley; however their presence extended as far east and south as the present-day Carolinas and Georgia. While socially organized under a matrilineal system, the Shawnee had male kings. Also Algonquin-speaking, the Delaware-based **Lenape** were considered by the Shawnee to be their "grandfathers" and thus accorded respect. Another Algonquin-speaking tribe, the **Kickapoo** were originally from the Great Lakes region but would move throughout present-day Indiana and Wisconsin. The **Miami** moved from Wisconsin to settle and farm in the Ohio Valley. They also took part in the fur trade.

THE SOUTHEAST

In the South, major tribes included the Chickasaw and Choctaw, the descendants of the **Mississippi Mound Builders** or Mississippian cultures, societies that built mounds from around 2,100 to 1,800 years ago as burial tombs or the bases for temples. Both tribes were organized in matrilineal clans, and both spoke Muskogean languages. The **Chickasaw** were based in northern Mississippi and Alabama and western Kentucky and Tennessee; they shared agricultural practices with the Iroquois. The **Choctaw**, whose origins trace to the Deep South and Florida, spoke a similar language to the Chickasaw. These two tribes would later form alliances with the British and French, fighting proxy wars on their behalf.

Figure 2.1. Mississippi Mounds

The **Creek**, also descended from the Mississippian peoples, originated in Alabama, Georgia, South Carolina, and Florida. The Muskogean-speaking Creek would later participate in an alliance with the Chickasaw and Choctaw—the Muscogee Confederacy—to engage the United States, which threatened tribal sovereignty.

Unlike the Chickasaw, Choctaw, and Creek, the **Cherokee** spoke (and speak) a language of the Iroquoian family. It is thought that they migrated south to their homeland in present-day Georgia sometime long before European contact, where they remained until they were forcibly removed in 1832. Organized into seven clans, the Cherokee were also hunters and farmers like other tribes in the region, and would later come into contact—and conflict—with European colonizers and the United States of America.

GREAT PLAINS, SOUTHWEST, PACIFIC NORTHWEST

Farther west, tribes of the Great Plains like the **Sioux**, **Cheyenne**, **Apache**, **Comanche**, and **Arapaho** would later come into conflict with American settlers during westward expansion. Traditionally nomadic or semi-nomadic, these tribes depended on the **buffalo** for food and materials; therefore they followed the herds.

In the Southwest, the **Navajo** controlled territory in present-day Arizona, New Mexico, and Utah. The Navajo were descendants of the cliff-dwelling **Ancestral Pueblo** or **Anasazi**, who had settled in the Four Corners area. The Navajo practiced pastoralism and lived in semi-permanent wooden homes called *hogans*. The Navajo had a less hierarchical structure than other Native American societies, and engaged in fewer raids than the Apache to the north.

Figure 2.2. Ancestral Pueblo Cliff Palace at Mesa Verde

In the Pacific Northwest, fishing was a major source of sustenance, and Native American peoples created and used canoes to engage in the practice. Totem poles depicted histories. The **Coast Salish**, whose language was widely spoken throughout the region, dominated the Puget Sound and Olympic Peninsula area. Farther south, the **Chinook** controlled the coast at the Columbia River.

Ultimately, through both violent conflict and political means, Native American civilizations lost control of most of their territories and were forced onto reservations by the United States. Negotiations continue today over rights to land and opportunities and reparations for past injustices.

SAMPLE QUESTIONS

1) **Which of the following best describes the political landscape of the Northeast before European contact?**

   A.   Many small, autonomous tribes scattered throughout the region fought over land and resources.

   B.   Several organized tribes controlled the region, including a major confederation.

   C.   A disorganized political landscape would facilitate European colonial domination.

   D.   The land was largely uninhabited, allowing easy exploitation of resources.

   Answer:

   B.   Correct. Powerful tribes controlled trade and territory; among these were the powerful Iroquois Confederacy.

2) **How do the movements of the tribes of the Northwest (throughout present-day Indiana, Illinois, Ohio, Michigan, and Wisconsin) illustrate tribal interactions before European contact and during colonial times?**

   A.   Having been pushed westward by the Iroquois, the Lenape are just one example of forced migration in early North American history.

   B.   The migration of the Miami from Ontario to the Ohio Valley illustrates the diffusion of the Algonquin language throughout the continent.

   C.   Despite the wide geographic range of the Shawnee, Kickapoo, Miami, and Lenape, all these peoples spoke variants of the Algonquin language; this shows the importance of this language for many Native American tribes whether or not they were Algonquin people.

   D.   Ongoing conflict between the Northwest Algonquin Confederacy, based in Ontario and the Upper Midwest, and the Iroquois Confederacy, based in the eastern Great Lakes region and present-day upstate New York, resulted in instability that forced tribes to move throughout the region.

   Answer:

   C.   Correct. While the Algonquin people were primarily located in what is today Quebec and southern Ontario, the Algonquin language was spoken widely throughout North America among both settled and semi-settled non-Algonquin peoples.

3) **At the time of European contact, the Southeastern United States was mainly populated by**

    A.   the Mississippi Mound Builders.

    B.   settled tribes who spoke Muskogean and Iroquoian languages.

    C.   nomadic tribes who spoke Muskogean and Iroquoian languages.

    D.   the Ancestral Pueblo cliff dwellers.

Answer:

    B.   **Correct.** The Choctaw, Creek, Chickasaw, and others were Muskogean-speaking peoples; the Cherokee spoke an Iroquoian language. Both tribes were settled.

4) **Tribes living in the Great Plains region were dependent on which of the following for survival?**

    A.   buffalo for nutrition and materials for daily necessities

    B.   domesticated horses for hunting and warfare

    C.   access to rivers to engage in the fur trade

    D.   three sisters agriculture

Answer:

    A.   **Correct.** The Great Plains tribes depended on buffalo, which were plentiful before European contact and settlement, for food; they also used buffalo parts for clothing and to make necessary items.

5) **How were the Navajo influenced by the Ancestral Pueblo, or Anasazi?**

    A.   The Navajo continued the practice of pastoralism, herding horses throughout the Southwest.

    B.   The Navajo expanded control over land originally settled by the Ancestral Pueblo.

    C.   The Navajo began building cliff dwellings, improving on the Anasazi practice of living in rounded homes built from wood.

    D.   The Navajo developed a strictly hierarchical society, abandoning the looser organization of the Ancestral Pueblo.

Answer:

    B.   **Correct.** The Ancestral Pueblo had settled in what is today the Four Corners region; the Navajo came to control land extending through present-day Arizona, New Mexico, and Utah.

Colonial North America

The Americas were quickly colonized by Europeans after Christopher Columbus first laid claim to them for the Spanish, and the British, French, and Spanish all held territories in North America throughout the sixteenth, seventeenth, eighteenth, and nineteenth centuries.

SPAIN IN THE WEST AND SOUTHWEST

Spanish *conquistadors* like **Hernando de Soto** and **Francisco Vasquez de Coronado** explored and conquered what is today the southwestern United States. Spanish colonization also meant spreading Christianity, so colonizers established **missions** throughout the region. The Spanish Crown granted *encomiendas*, land grants to individuals to establish settlements, allowing the holder to ranch or mine the land. Colonists demanded tribute and forced labor from local Native peoples, essentially enslaving them, to profit from the land. Spain's holdings ultimately extended through the Southwest, parts of the Rocky Mountains, and California. Spain also controlled the Gulf Coast, including New Orleans and Florida.

Throughout this region, Spanish colonizers encountered resistance from Native Americans. Spain temporarily lost land for two years after the 1680 **Pueblo Revolt**. Sometimes referred to as part of the ongoing **Navajo Wars**, this revolt included several Native American tribes. Spain eventually reconquered the territory, subjugating the peoples living in the region to colonial rule.

The conflict led to friction among Spanish thinkers over the means, and even the notion, of colonization. The priest **Bartolomé de las Casas**, who lived in the Americas, was appalled at the oppression of colonization and argued for the rights and humanity of Native Americans. On the other hand, **Juan de Sepulveda**, who never left Spain, argued that the Native Americans needed the rule and "civilization" brought by Spain, justifying their treatment at the hands of colonizers.

Despite ongoing conflict between Native Americans and Spanish colonizers, there was social mixing among the people. Intermarriage and fraternization resulted in a stratified society based on race in Spanish and Portuguese colonies throughout the Western Hemisphere. According to the *casta* system, race determined an individual's place in the societal hierarchy, with white people most privileged. The term *mestizo* referred to people of mixed white European and Native American, who were more privileged than the Native American peoples.

The Spanish also introduced African people to the Americas. Forced labor and diseases like **smallpox** had decimated Native American populations in Mexico and the Southwest. Consequently, in order to exploit these resource-rich lands, Spanish colonizers took part in the European-driven **trans-Atlantic slave trade**, kidnapping African people or purchasing them on the West African coast, bringing them to the Americas and forcing them into slavery in mines and plantations.

FRENCH HEGEMONY IN THE MIDWEST AND NORTHEAST

Unlike Spain, which sought not only profit but also to settle the land and convert Native Americans to Christianity, France was mainly focused on trade. **Jacques**

Cartier claimed New France (Quebec) for France in the sixteenth century. French explorers like **Samuel de Champlain** reached land in Vermont, northern New York, and the eastern Great Lakes region, consolidating control of France's North American colonies in 1608.

European demand was high for **fur** and beaver pelts from the Northeast. French colonists were also more likely to establish agreements and intermarry with local Native Americans than other European powers; they did not establish settlements based on forced labor or arrive with families. The term *métis* described mixed-race persons. Eventually France would control the valuable trade routes throughout the Great Lakes and the Mississippi region through Louisiana and New Orleans.

ENGLAND AND THE THIRTEEN COLONIES

Unlike the Spanish and French, the English brought their families to North America, with the goal of establishing agricultural settlements. In the sixteenth century, Sir Walter Raleigh established the Roanoke colony in present-day Virginia; while this settlement mysteriously disappeared by 1590, interest in colonization reemerged as **joint-stock companies** sought royal charters to privately develop colonies on the North American Atlantic coast. The first established colony, **Jamestown**, was also located in Virginia, and became so profitable that the Crown took it over in 1624.

Tobacco was the primary cash crop in Virginia. Since tobacco grew on plantations, Virginia required **indentured servants** to farm it. These workers were freed from servitude after a period of work. Some did come from Africa. However in 1660, the **House of Burgesses**, which governed Virginia, declared that all blacks would be lifelong slaves even if they had been indentured servants. The South became increasingly socially stratified, with enslaved persons, indentured servants, land-owners, and other classes. The Carolinas and Georgia would also become important sources of tobacco (and rice); South Carolina institutionalized slavery in North America for the next two centuries by adopting the slave codes from Barbados.

While Jamestown and Virginia were populated by diverse groups of settlers, businessmen, indentured servants, and slaves, the demographics were different farther north. In New England, **Separatists**, members of the Church of England who believed it had strayed too far from its theological roots, had come to North America seeking more religious freedom. The first group of Separatists, the Pilgrims, arrived on the *Mayflower* in 1620 and had

> **DID YOU KNOW?**
>
> Slavery was not as widespread in the northern colonies as it was in the South, as the climate in the North did not support plantation agriculture. Demand for slaves was therefore higher in the South, where unskilled labor was needed to harvest tobacco and later, cotton.

drawn up the **Mayflower Compact**, guaranteeing government by the consent of the governed. They were later joined by the **Puritans**, who had been persecuted in England. The colonial Puritan leader **John Winthrop** envisioned the Massachusetts

Bay Colony in the model of the biblical *City upon a Hill*, rooted in unity, peace, and what would be a free, democratic spirit. These philosophies would later inform the American Revolution.

A form of social stratification existed in New England as well: according to Puritan belief, wealth and success showed that one was a member of the **elect**, or privileged by God. Poorer farmers were generally tenant farmers; they did not own land and rarely made a profit.

The concepts of religious tolerance were not isolated to New England. The mid-Atlantic region was well suited for agriculture and trade, with fertile lands and natural harbors. The commercial settlement of New Amsterdam came under English control in 1664 and was renamed New York; in 1682, the Quaker **William Penn** founded the city of Philadelphia. Pennsylvania, New Jersey, and Delaware were founded in the Quaker spirit as part of Penn's **Holy Experiment** to develop settlements based on tolerance.

DID YOU KNOW?

Quakerism promotes equality, community, non-violence, conflict resolution, and tolerance. These ideas are at the root of the name of Philadelphia, the "City of Brotherly Love."

Earlier in the region, in 1649 the **Maryland Toleration Act** had ensured the political rights of all Christians there, the first law of its kind in the colonies. This was due, in part, to the influence of **Lord Baltimore**, who had been charged by Charles I to found a part of Virginia (to be called Maryland) as a Catholic haven—helping him maintain power in an England divided between Catholics and Protestants.

The North American colonial economy was part of the **Atlantic World**, taking part in the **Triangular Trade** among the Americas, Africa, and Europe, where slaves were exchanged in the Americas for raw materials and goods, raw materials were shipped to Europe to be processed into goods for the benefit of the colonial powers, and these goods were sometimes exchanged for slaves in Africa. In this way, North America was part of the **Columbian Exchange**, the intersection of goods and people throughout the Atlantic World.

Exploitation of colonial resources and the dynamics of the Columbian Exchange supported **mercantilism**, the prevailing economic system: European powers controlled their economies in order to increase global power. Ensuring a beneficial **balance of trade** is essential; the country must export more than it imports. An unlimited supply of desirable goods obtainable at a low cost made this possible, and the colonies offered just that. In this way, European powers would be able to maintain their reserves of gold and silver rather than spending them on imports. Furthermore, those countries that obtained access to more gold and silver—notably, Spain, which gained control of mines in Central America and Mexico— exponentially increased their wealth, dramatically changing the balance of economic power in Europe. Long-term consequences included the decline of feudalism and the rise of capitalism.

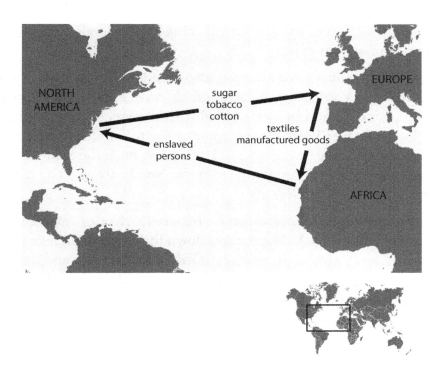

Figure 2.3. Triangular Trade

COLONIAL CONFLICT

Throughout the chaos in England during the **English Civil War**, policy toward the colonies had been one of **salutary neglect**, allowing them great autonomy. However, stability in England and an emerging culture of independence in the Thirteen Colonies caught the attention of the British Crown. To protect the British mercantilist system, the **Navigation Acts** were enacted in 1651, forbidding colonial trade with any other countries. **Bacon's Rebellion** against the colonial governor of Virginia in 1676 embodied the growing resentment of landowners, who wanted to profit rather than redirect revenue to Britain. Following the 1688 Glorious Revolution in England, many colonists expected more autonomy; however, new leadership continued to limit self-rule.

American colonists were also increasingly influenced by Enlightenment thought. John Locke's *Second Treatise* was published in 1689; critical of absolute monarchy, it became popular in the colonies. Locke's concepts of government by consent of the governed and the natural rights of persons became the bedrock of the United States government. Locke argued for **republicanism**: that the people must come together to create a government for the protection of themselves and their property, thereby giving up some of their natural rights. However, should the government overstep its bounds, the people have the right to overthrow it and replace it.

In the mid-eighteenth century, a sense of religious fervor called the **Great Awakening** spread throughout the colonies; people became devoted to God beyond the confines of traditional Christianity. Many universities were founded during this time to train ministers; the Great Awakening helped develop a more singularly North American religious culture.

Meanwhile, North America served also as a battleground for France and England, already in conflict in Europe and elsewhere. In the mid-seventeenth century, the Algonquin and Iroquois, allied with the French and English, respectively, fought the **Beaver Wars** for control over the fur trade in the northeastern part of the continent. The Iroquois would ultimately push the Shawnee and other tribes associated with the Algonquin from the Northeast and Great Lakes area farther west to present-day Wisconsin.

France had come to control the vast **Louisiana Territory**, from the Ohio Valley area through the Mississippi Valley, the area down the Mississippi River to its capital of New Orleans, and as far as the reaches of the Missouri River and the Arkansas/Red River stretching west. Not only did France clash with Britain in the northern part of the continent, but the two colonial powers came into conflict in the South as well. In 1736, French forces, allied with the Choctaw, attacked the English-allied Chickasaw as part of France's attempts to strengthen its hold on the southeastern part of North America in the **Chickasaw Wars**.

Figure 2.4. *Join, or Die.*

Following another period of salutary neglect in the colonies, in 1754, French and English conflict exploded once again in North America as fighting broke out in the Ohio Valley. The British government organized with North American colonial leaders to meet at Albany; **Benjamin Franklin** helped organize the defensive Albany Plan of Union and argued for this plan in his newspaper, the *Pennsylvania Gazette*, using the famous illustration *Join, or Die*. However, the Crown worried that this plan allowed for too much colonial independence, adding to tensions between the Thirteen Colonies and England.

The Seven Years' War broke out in Europe in 1756; this conflict between the British and French in North America was known as the **French and Indian War**. War efforts in North America accelerated; ultimately, Britain emerged as the dominant power on the continent. France had allied with the Algonquin, traditional rivals of the British-allied Iroquois. However, following defeats by strong colonial military leaders like **George Washington** and despite its strong alliances and long-term presence on the continent, France eventually surrendered. Britain gained control of French territories in North America—as well as Spanish Florida—in the 1763 **Treaty of Paris** which ended the Seven Years' War.

SAMPLE QUESTIONS

6) **How did Spanish and French colonization in North America differ?**

    A.   Both intermarried with Native Americans; however the Spanish took a more aggressive approach in spreading Christianity.

    B.   Spain sought accord and agreement with Native Americans, while France forced marriages as part of settling the land.

    C.   France colonized the Southwest; Spain colonized the Northeast and Midwest.

    D.   France imported enslaved Africans as part of the Triangular Trade in order to support New France, while Spain mainly exploited the labor of local Native American tribes.

    Answer:

    A.   **Correct.** Spain established missions to spread Christianity, in addition to settling and exploiting the land; France worked to establish networks of trade and did not concentrate on religious conversion (although the Church was present and at work in its colonies). Both intermarried locally.

7) **On the Atlantic coast of North America, which of the following contributed to demographic differences between North and South?**

    A.   a climate that supported plantation agriculture in the southern colonies, which resulted in high demand for African slaves

    B.   geography favorable to ports in the Northeast, resulting in diverse and tolerant centers of commerce and trade in Boston, New York, and Philadelphia

    C.   a climate that supported small-scale agriculture and family farms in the northern colonies, which resulted in a very low demand for African slaves

    D.   all of the above

Answer:

D.   Correct. All of the above answer choices are true.

8)   **The mid-Atlantic colonies of Pennsylvania, Delaware, and New Jersey were founded on what premise?**

A.   to be a beacon of unity and humanity, reminiscent of John Winthrop's *City upon a Hill*

B.   to reflect tolerance, as part of William Penn's *Holy Experiment*

C.   to turn a profit, in accordance with their roots in joint-stock companies seeking royal charters

D.   to conquer land and convert Native American tribes to Christianity

Answer:

B.   Correct. William Penn founded these colonies in the spirit of his tolerant Quaker faith.

9)   **How did the British and French rivalry spill over into North America?**

A.   While Britain and France were often on opposite sides in European conflict, they found common ground against Native Americans in North America.

B.   European conflicts between Catholics and Protestants affected Catholic French and Protestant English settlers; related violence from the Hundred Years' War broke out between them as a result.

C.   These European powers engaged in proxy wars, supporting powerful tribes jockeying for control of land in the Great Lakes and southeastern regions of North America.

D.   France and Britain formed an alliance to prevent Spain from moving eastward on the continent.

Answer:

C.   Correct. The Beaver Wars, the Chickasaw Wars, and later the French and Indian War, which was part of the Seven Years' War, are all examples of British-French conflict playing out in North America.

10)   **Which of the following were factors in stirring up colonial discontent?**

A.   Locke's *Second Treatise*

B.   trade restrictions like the Navigation Acts

C.   the Great Awakening

D.   all of the above

Answer:

D.   Correct. All of the above are true.

Revolution and the Early United States

The American Revolution

Despite British victory in the French and Indian War, Britain had gone into debt. Furthermore, there were concerns that the colonies required a stronger military presence following **Pontiac's Rebellion** in 1763. The leader of the **Ottawa** people, Pontiac, led a revolt that extended from the Great Lakes region through the Ohio Valley to Virginia. As this land had been ceded to England from France (lacking any consultation with the native inhabitants) the Ottawa people and other Native Americans resisted further British settlement and fought back against colonial oppression. **King George III** signed the **Proclamation of 1763**, an agreement not to settle land west of the Appalachians, in an effort to make peace; however much settlement continued in practice.

As a result of the war and subsequent unrest, Britain once again discarded its colonial policy of salutary neglect; furthermore, in desperate need of cash, the Crown sought ways to increase its revenue from the colonies.

King George III enforced heavy taxes and restrictive acts in the colonies to generate income for the Crown and punish disobedience. England expanded the **Molasses Act** of 1733, passing the **Sugar Act** in 1764 to raise revenue by taxing sugar and molasses. Sugar was produced in the British West Indies and widely consumed in the Thirteen Colonies. In 1765, Britain enforced the **Quartering Act**, requiring colonists to provide shelter to British troops stationed in the region.

The 1765 **Stamp Act**, the first direct tax on the colonists, triggered more tensions. Any document required a costly stamp, the revenue reverting to the British government. **Patrick Henry** protested the Stamp Act in the Virginia House of Burgesses; the tax was seen as a violation of colonists' rights, given that they did not have direct representation in British Parliament. In Britain, it was argued that the colonists had **virtual representation** and so the Act—and others to follow—were justified.

As a result, colonists began boycotting British goods and engaging in violent protest. **Samuel Adams** led the **Sons and Daughters of Liberty** in violent acts against tax collectors. In response, the Chancellor of the Exchequer Charles Townshend enforced the punitive **Townshend Acts** which imposed more taxes and restrictions on the colonies; customs officers were empowered to search colonists' homes for forbidden goods with **writs of assistance**. John Dickinson's *Letters from a Farmer in Pennsylvania* and Samuel Adams' **Massachusetts Circular Letter** argued for the repeal of the Townshend Acts (which were, indeed, repealed in 1770) and demanded *no taxation without representation*. Samuel Adams continued to stir up rebellion with his **Committees of Correspondence**, which distributed anti-British propaganda.

Protests against the Quartering Act in Boston led to the **Boston Massacre** in 1770, when British troops fired on a crowd of protesters. By 1773, in a climate of continued unrest driven by the Committees of Correspondence, colonists protested the latest taxes on tea levied by the **Tea Act** in the famous **Boston Tea**

Party by dressing as Native Americans and tossing tea off a ship in Boston Harbor. In response, the government passed the **Intolerable Acts**, closing Boston Harbor and bringing Massachusetts back under direct royal control.

In response to the Intolerable Acts, colonial leaders met in Philadelphia at the **First Continental Congress** in 1774 and issued the *Declaration of Rights and Grievances*, presenting colonial concerns to the King, who ignored it. However, violent conflict began in 1775 at **Lexington and Concord**, when American militiamen (**minutemen**) had gathered to resist British efforts to seize weapons and arrest rebels in Concord. On June 17, 1775, the Americans fought the British at the **Battle of Bunker Hill**; despite American losses, the number of casualties the rebels inflicted caused the king to declare that the colonies were in rebellion. Troops were deployed to the colonies; the Siege of Boston began.

DID YOU KNOW?

King George III also hired Hessian mercenaries from Germany to supplement British troops; adding foreign fighters only increased resentment in the colonies and created a stronger sense of independence from Britain.

In May 1775, the **Second Continental Congress** met at Philadelphia to debate the way forward. Debate between the wisdom of continued efforts at compromise and negotiations and declaring independence continued. The king ignored the Congress's *Declaration of the Causes and Necessities of Taking Up Arms*, which asked him to consider again the colonies' objections; he also ignored the **Olive Branch Petition** which sought compromise and an end to hostilities. **Thomas Paine** published his pamphlet *Common Sense*; taking Locke's concepts of natural rights and the obligation of a people to rebel against an oppressive government, it popularized the notion of rebellion against Britain.

By summer of 1776, the Continental Congress agreed on the need to break from Britain; on July 4, 1776, it declared the independence of the United States of America and issued the **Declaration of Independence**, drafted mainly by **Thomas Jefferson** and heavily influenced by Locke.

Americans were still divided over independence; **Patriots** favored independence while those still loyal to Britain were known as **Tories**. **George Washington** had been appointed head of the Continental Army and led a largely unpaid and unprofessional army; despite early losses, Washington gained ground due to strong leadership, superior knowledge of the land, and support from France (and to a lesser extent, Spain and the Netherlands). The tide turned in 1777 at **Valley Forge**, when Washington and his army lived through the bitterly cold winter and managed to overcome British military forces. The British people did not favor the war and voted the Tories out of Parliament; the incoming Whig party sought to end the war. In the 1783 **Treaty of Paris**, the United States was recognized as a country, agreeing to repay debts to British merchants and provide safety to those British loyalists who wished to remain in North America. The American Revolution would go on to inspire revolution around the world.

FEDERALISTS AND DEMOCRATIC-REPUBLICANS

Joy in victory was short-lived. Fearful of tyranny, the Second Continental Congress had authorized only a weak central government, adopting the **Articles of Confederation** to organize the Thirteen Colonies—now states—into a loosely united country. A unicameral central government had the power to wage war, negotiate treaties, and borrow money. It could not tax citizens, but it could tax states. It also set parameters for westward expansion and establishing new states: the **Northwest Ordinances** of 1787 forbade slavery north of the Ohio River. Areas with 60,000 people could apply for statehood. However, it soon became clear that the Articles of Confederation were not strong enough to keep the nation united.

The new country was heavily in debt. Currency was weak, taxes were high, and instability loomed. Daniel Shays led **Shays' Rebellion**, a revolt of indebted farmers who sought to prevent courts from seizing property in Massachusetts and to protest debtor's prisons. Furthermore, debt and disorganization made the country appear weak and vulnerable to Great Britain and Spain. If the United States was to remain one country, it needed a stronger federal government.

> **DID YOU KNOW?**
>
> The Northwest Ordinances also effectively nullified King George III's Proclamation of 1763, which promised Native Americans that white settlement would not continue in the Ohio Valley region. The United States did not recognize the Proclamation, and tensions would build.

Alexander Hamilton and **James Madison** called for a **Constitutional Convention** to frame a stronger federal government in a written constitution. Madison and other **Federalists** like **John Adams** believed in **separation of powers**, republicanism, and a strong federal government.

To determine the exact structure of the government, delegates at the convention settled on what became known as the **Great Compromise**, a **bicameral legislature**. Two plans had been presented: the **New Jersey Plan**, which proposed a legislature composed of an equal number of representatives from each state (which would benefit smaller states), and the **Virginia Plan**, which proposed a legislature composed of representatives proportional to the population of each state. States with large populations of enslaved African Americans accounted for those persons with the **Three-Fifths Compromise**, which counted a slave as three-fifths of a person. While represented in a state's population to determine that state's representation in Congress, enslaved persons had no place in the political process. The states adopted both plans, creating the **House of Representatives** and the **Senate**, to represent the large and small states at the federal level.

Despite the separation of powers provided for in the Constitution, **Anti-Federalists** like **Thomas Jefferson** called for even more limitations on the power of the federal government. The first ten amendments to the Constitution, or the **Bill of Rights**, a list of guarantees of American freedoms, was a concession to the

Anti-Federalists, who would later become the **Democratic-Republican Party** (eventually, the Democratic Party).

To convince the states of the benefits of federalism and to ratify the Constitution, Hamilton, Madison, and John Jay wrote the *Federalist Papers*. Likewise, the Bill of Rights helped sway the hesitant. In 1791, the Constitution was ratified. **George Washington** was elected president, with John Adams serving as vice president; Washington appointed Hamilton as Secretary of the Treasury and Jefferson as Secretary of State.

Hamilton prioritized currency stabilization and repayment of debts; he also believed in establishing a national bank—the **Bank of the United States (BUS)**. He also favored tariffs and excise (sales) taxes, which Anti-Federalists—who became known as **Democratic-Republicans**—vehemently opposed. in 1795, rebellion against the excise tax on whiskey broke out; the **Whiskey Rebellion** indicated unrest in the young country and was put down by militia.

President Washington issued the **Neutrality Proclamation** in 1793, keeping the US out of the French Revolution. However, British and French ships accosted American ships in the Atlantic and forced American sailors into naval service (**impressment**). **Jay's Treaty**, an attempt at reinstating neutrality, was unsuccessful and unpopular; it only negotiated the removal of British forts in the western frontier. Furthermore, Spain became concerned about changes in the continental balance of power. President Washington had Thomas Pickney negotiate a new treaty with Spain; giving the US rights on the Mississippi River and in the Port of New Orleans, **Pickney's Treaty** was a diplomatic success and ratified by all thirteen states. The **Northwest Indian Wars** continued in the Ohio region; ultimately the Americans gained territory in Ohio and Indiana following the defeat of allied tribes at the **Battle of Fallen Timbers** in 1794.

> **DID YOU KNOW?**
>
> Federalists were generally from the North and were usually merchants or businessmen; Anti-Federalists were usually from the South or the rural west, and farmed the land.

In President Washington's **Farewell Address**, he recommended the United States adhere to neutrality in international affairs, setting a precedent for early American history. Vice President John Adams, a Federalist, became the second president. France continued to seize American ships, so Adams sent representatives to negotiate; however, in what became known as the **XYZ Affair**, the Americans were asked for bribes in order to even meet with French officials. The insulted Americans began an undeclared conflict in the Caribbean until the **Convention of 1800** negotiated a cessation of hostilities.

During the Adams administration, the Federalists passed the harsh **Alien and Sedition Acts**. The Alien Act allowed the president to deport "enemy aliens"; it also increased the residency requirements for citizenship. The Sedition Act forbade criticism of the president or of Congress. Divisions between the Federalists and the Democratic-Republicans were deeper than ever and the presidential elections of 1800 were tense and controversial. Nevertheless, Thomas Jefferson was elected to the presidency in 1801 in a non-violent transfer of power.

Jefferson repealed the Alien and Sedition Acts and shrank the federal government. Economic policies favored small farmers and landowners, in contrast to Federalist policies, which supported big business and cities. However, Jefferson also oversaw the **Louisiana Purchase**, which nearly doubled the size of the United States. This troubled some Democratic-Republicans, who saw this as federal overreach, but the Louisiana Purchase would be a major step in westward expansion.

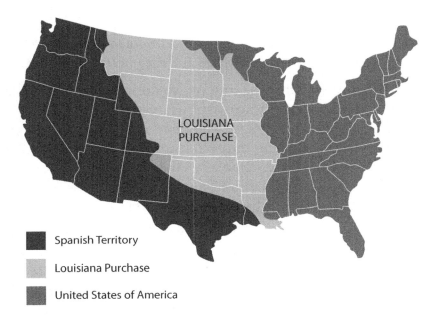

Figure 2.5. Louisiana Purchase

Jefferson was also forced to manage chaotic international affairs. Britain and France, at war in Europe, were attempting to blockade each other's international trade, threatening US ships and commerce. In an attempt to avoid the conflict, Congress passed the **Embargo Act** in 1807, restricting international trade. However this law only damaged the US economy further. At the end of Jefferson's presidency, Congress passed the **Non-Intercourse Act**, which allowed trade with foreign countries besides Britain and France; under President **James Madison**, tensions would remain high.

Monroe Doctrine and Manifest Destiny

British provocation at sea and in the northwest led to the **War of 1812**. Growing nationalism in the United States pressured Madison into pushing for war after the **Battle of Tippecanoe** in Indiana, when **General William Henry Harrison** fought the **Northwest Confederacy**, a group of tribes led by the Shawnee leader **Tecumseh**. The Shawnee, Lenape, Miami, Kickapoo, and others had come together not only out of common interest—to maintain control over their lands—but also because they followed Tecumseh's brother **Tenskwatawa**, who was considered a prophet.

Despite the Confederacy's alliance with Britain, the United States prevailed. Congress declared war with the intent to defend the United States, end commercial disruption and impressment of Americans at sea, and destabilize British Canada. The war resulted in no real gains or losses for either the Americans or the British. Yet at the war's end, the United States had successfully reaffirmed its independence. The Federalists, who had opposed the war, eventually collapsed. Patriotism ran high.

The **Era of Good Feelings** began with the presidency of **James Monroe** as a strong sense of public identity and nationalism pervaded in the country. In a religious revival called the **Second Great Awakening**, people turned from Puritanism to Baptist and Methodist faiths, following revolutionary preachers and movements. In art and culture, romanticism and reform movements elevated the "common man," a trend that would continue into the presidency of Andrew Jackson.

From a financial perspective, the country would again struggle. Disagreement over the **Tariff of 1816** divided industrialists, who believed in nurturing American industry, from Southern landowners, who depended on exporting cotton and tobacco for profit. Later, following the establishment of the **Second Bank of the United States**, the **Panic of 1819** erupted when the government cut credit following overspeculation on western lands; the BUS wanted payment from state banks in hard currency, or **specie**. Western banks foreclosed on western farmers.

With the Louisiana Purchase, the country had almost doubled in size. In the nineteenth century, the idea of **manifest destiny**, or the sense that it was the fate of the United States to expand westward and settle the continent, prevailed. Also in 1819, the United States purchased Florida from Spain in the **Adams-Onis Treaty**. The **Monroe Doctrine**, James Monroe's policy that the Western Hemisphere was "closed" to any further European colonization or exploration, asserted US hegemony in the region.

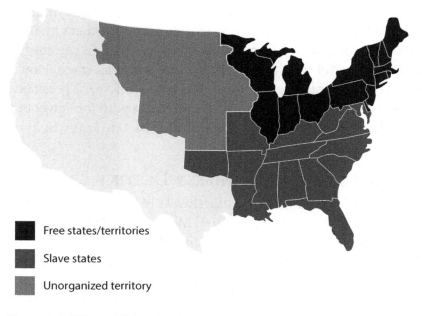

■ Free states/territories

■ Slave states

■ Unorganized territory

Figure 2.6. Missouri Compromise

Westward expansion triggered questions about the expansion of slavery, a divisive issue. Slavery was profitable for the southern states which depended on the plantation economy, but increasingly condemned in the North. Furthermore, the Second Great Awakening had fueled the **abolitionist** movement. In debating the nature of westward expansion, the Kentucky senator **Henry Clay** worked out a compromise. The **Missouri Compromise**, also known as the **Compromise of 1820**, allowed Missouri to join the union as a slave state, but provided that any other states north of the **thirty-sixth parallel (36°30′)** would be free. Maine would also join the nation as a free state. However, more tension and compromises over the nature of slavery in the West were to come.

Jacksonian Democracy

Demographics were changing throughout the early nineteenth century. Technological advances had increased cotton yield; therefore, more persons were enslaved than ever before, bringing more urgency to the issue of slavery. In addition, **immigration** from Europe to the United States was increasing. Reactionary **nativist** movements like the **Know-Nothing Party** feared the influx of non-Anglo Europeans, particularly Catholics, and discrimination was widespread, especially against the Irish. Other technological advances like the **railroads** and **steamships** were speeding up westward expansion and improving trade throughout the continent; a large-scale **market economy** was emerging. With early industrialization and changing concepts following the Second Great Awakening, women were playing a larger role in society, even though they could not vote.

Most states had extended voting rights to white men who did not own land or substantial property: **universal manhood suffrage**. Elected officials would increasingly come to better reflect the electorate, and the brash war hero Jackson was popular among the "common man."

During the election of 1824, Andrew Jackson ran against **John Quincy Adams**, Henry Clay, and William Crawford, all Republicans (from the Democratic-Republican party); John Quincy Adams won. By 1828, divisions within the party had Jackson and his supporters known as Democrats, in favor of small farmers and inhabitants of rural areas, and states' rights. Clay and his supporters became known as **National Republicans** and, later, **Whigs**, a splinter group of the Democratic-Republicans which supported business and urbanization; they also had federalist leanings. Thus the **two-party system** emerged.

Andrew Jackson's popularity with the "common man," white, male farmers and workers who felt he identified with them, and the fact that owning property was no longer a requirement to vote, gave him the advantage and a two-term presidency. Jackson rewarded his supporters, appointing them to important positions as part of the **spoils system**.

Opposed to the Bank of the United States, he issued the **Specie Circular**, devaluing paper money and instigating the financial **Panic of 1837**. Despite his opposition to such deep federal economic control, Jackson was forced to contend with controversial tariffs. The **Tariff of 1828**, or **Tariff of Abominations**, benefitted northern industry, but heavily affected southern exports. Senator **John C. Calhoun** of South Carolina argued for **nullification**, the right of a state to declare a law null and void if it was harmful.

Tensions increased with the **Tariff of 1832**; Calhoun and South Carolina threatened to secede if their economic interests were not protected. Jackson managed the **Nullification Crisis** without resorting to violence, working out a compromise in 1833 that was more favorable to the South.

Socially and politically, white men of varying levels of economic success and education had stronger political voices and more opportunities in civil society. However, women, African Americans, and Native Americans did not. With continental expansion came conflict with Native Americans. Despite efforts by the Cherokee, who unsuccessfully argued for the right to their land in the Supreme Court case *Cherokee Nation v. Georgia* (1831), President Jackson enforced the 1830 **Indian Removal Act**, forcing tribes from their lands in the Southeast. Thousands of people were forced to travel mainly on foot, with all of their belongings, to Indian Territory (today, Oklahoma) on the infamous **Trail of Tears**, to make way for white settlers. Violent conflicts would continue on the Frontier farther west between the US and the Apache, Comanche, Sioux, Arapaho, Cheyenne, and other tribes throughout the nineteenth century.

SAMPLE QUESTIONS

11) **How did the Quartering Act impact the colonists?**

  A.   Colonists were forced to take British soldiers into their homes; protests against the Act led to the Boston Tea Party.

  B.   Colonists were forced to build quarters for British soldiers who were stationed locally.

  C.   Colonists had to provide one-quarter of their earnings to support British soldiers stationed locally.

  D.   Colonists were forced to take British soldiers into their homes; protests against the Act led to the Boston Massacre.

Answer:

  D.   Correct. Anger at being forced to provide shelter for British soldiers led to protests; in 1770, British soldiers fired on protests against the Quartering Act in what came to be called the Boston Massacre.

12) **What was the impact of Shays' Rebellion?**

A.   It showed resistance to imposing excise taxes on whiskey and other consumer goods.

B.   It illustrated the need for a stronger federal government in the young United States.

C.   Taxes engineered by Hamilton during the Washington administration were cut.

D.   The radical Democratic-Republicans emerged to protest the Bank of the United States.

Answer:

B.   **Correct.** Shays' Rebellion, in which Daniel Shays led a rebellion of indebted farmers shortly after the end of the Revolution, showed the need for a stronger federal government to ensure national stability and was a major factor in planning the Constitutional Convention.

13) **What was the impact of United States' rejection of the Proclamation of 1763?**

A.   A series of conflicts between the Americans and the Northwest tribes (later, the Northwest Confederacy) culminated in the War of 1812. Ultimately, the US would control the land.

B.   The French and British formed the Northwest Confederacy, allying against the United States to control more land in North America.

C.   A series of conflicts between the Americans and the Northwest tribes culminated in the War of 1812. Ultimately, the Northwest Confederacy would control the land for another century before ceding it to Canada.

D.   The Northwest Confederacy of British and American soldiers united to drive Native American tribes from what is today the Midwest region of the United States, allowing whites to establish settlements there.

Answer:

A.   **Correct.** Despite efforts by the tribes to retain control over their land, they would eventually lose a series of conflicts and the United States would establish states in the Midwest and Ohio Valley region.

14) **How did the Missouri Compromise reflect divisions over slavery?**

A.   It showed disagreement over the nature of westward expansion.

B.   It showed the impact of the abolitionist movement on politics.

C.   It showed how the Second Great Awakening had influenced society.

D.   all of the above

Answer:

D.   **Correct.** All of the answer choices are true.

15) **How did demographics play a part in democratic change during the early and mid-nineteenth century, particularly in the context of Jacksonian Democracy?**

   A.   The rising strength of industry in the Northeast, coupled with the beginnings of railroads, strengthened support for pro-business politicians and the business class.

   B.   Wealthy European immigrants shifted the balance of power away from the "common man" to business owners and the elites, leading to the rise of the powerful Whig party.

   C.   Universal manhood suffrage shifted the balance of political power away from the elites; immigration accelerated westward expansion and began to power early industry and urban development.

   D.   Jackson's focus on strengthening the federal government dissatisfied the South, leading to the Nullification Crisis.

Answer:

   C.   Correct. Universal manhood suffrage allowed all white males, whether or not they owned property, to vote; the "common man" had a voice in government, and Jackson enjoyed their support. Likewise, an influx of poor European immigrants changed the country's demographics, providing more workers for early industry, more settlers to populate the west, and a stronger voice in government against the wealthy.

CIVIL WAR, EXPANSION, AND INDUSTRY

THE ROAD TO CONFLICT

The Civil War was rooted in ongoing conflict over slavery, states' rights, and the reach of the federal government. Reform movements of the mid-nineteenth century fueled the abolitionist movement. The Missouri Compromise and the Nullification Crisis foreshadowed worsening division to come.

In 1836, Texas, where there were a great number of white settlers, declared independence from Mexico. In 1845, Texas joined the Union; this event, in addition to US hunger for land, triggered the **Mexican-American War**. As a result of the **Treaty of Guadalupe Hidalgo**, which ended the war following Mexico's surrender, the United States obtained territory in the Southwest and gold-rich California. The population of California would grow rapidly with the **gold rush** as prospectors headed west to try their fortunes. However, Hispanics who had lived in the region under Mexico lost their land and were denied many of the rights that whites enjoyed—even though they had been promised US citizenship and equal rights under the treaty. They also suffered from racial discrimination.

Meanwhile, social change in the Northeast and growing Midwest continued. As the market economy and early industry developed, so did the **middle class**. The role of **women** changed; extra income allowed many to stay at home. The

Cult of Domesticity, a popular cultural movement, encouraged women to become homemakers and focus on domestic skills. However, women were also freed up to engage in social activism. Activists like **Susan B. Anthony** and **Elizabeth Cady Stanton** worked for women's rights, including women's suffrage, culminating in the 1848 **Seneca Falls Convention** led by the **American Woman Suffrage Association**. Women were also active in the temperance movement. Organizations like the Woman's Christian Temperance Union advocated for the prohibition of alcohol, which was finally achieved with the Eighteenth Amendment, although it was later repealed with the Twenty-First.

Reform movements continued to include abolitionism, which ranged from moderate to radical. The American Colonization Society wanted to end slavery and send former slaves to Africa. The activist, writer, and former slave **Frederick Douglass** advocated for **abolition**. Douglass publicized the movement along with the American Anti-Slavery Society and publications like Harriet Beecher Stowe's *Uncle Tom's Cabin*. The radical abolitionist **John Brown** led violent protests against slavery. Abolitionism became a key social and political issue.

The industrial change in the North did not extend to the South, which continued to rely on plantations and cotton exports. Nor were the majority of demographic changes occurring in the South. Differences among the regions grew, and disputes over extending slavery into new southwestern territories obtained from Mexico continued. Another compromise was needed.

Anti-slavery factions in Congress had attempted to halt the extension of slavery to the new territories obtained from Mexico in the 1846 **Wilmot Proviso**, but these efforts were unsuccessful. The later **Compromise of 1850** admitted the populous California as a free state and Utah and New Mexico to the Union with slavery to be decided by **popular sovereignty**, or by the residents. It also reaffirmed the **Fugitive Slave Act**, which allowed slave owners to pursue escaped slaves to free states and recapture them. It would now be a federal crime to assist escaped slaves, an unacceptable provision to many abolitionists.

Shortly thereafter, Congress passed the **Kansas-Nebraska Act of 1854** which allowed those two territories to decide slavery by popular sovereignty as well, effectively repealing the Missouri Compromise. A new party, the **Republican Party**, was formed by angered Democrats, Whigs, and others as a result; later, one of its members, Abraham Lincoln, would be elected to the presidency. Violence broke out in Kansas between pro- and anti-slavery factions in what became known as **Bleeding Kansas**.

In 1856, an escaped slave, **Dred Scott**, took his case to the Supreme Court to sue for freedom. Scott had escaped to the free state of Illinois and sought to stay there; his former "owner" had argued that he could get him back regardless of the state he was in. The Court heard the case, *Scott v. Sandford*, and ruled in favor of Sandford, upholding the Fugitive Slave Act, the Kansas-Nebraska Act, and nullifying the Missouri Compromise. The Court essentially decreed that African Americans were not entitled to rights under US citizenship.

In 1858, a series of debates between Illinois Senate candidates, Republican **Abraham Lincoln** and Democrat **Stephen Douglas**, showed the deep divides in the nation over slavery and states' rights. During the **Lincoln-Douglas Debates**, Lincoln spoke out against slavery, while Douglas supported the right of states to decide its legality on their own. In 1860, Lincoln was elected to the presidency. Given his outspoken stance against slavery, South Carolina seceded immediately, followed by Mississippi, Alabama, Florida, Louisiana, Georgia, and Texas. They formed the Confederate States of America, or the **Confederacy**, on February 1, 1861, under the leadership of **Jefferson Davis**, a senator from Mississippi.

Shortly after the South's secession, Confederate forces attacked Union troops in Charleston Harbor, South Carolina; the **Battle of Fort Sumter** sparked the Civil War. As a result, Virginia, Tennessee, North Carolina, and Arkansas seceded and joined the Confederacy. West Virginia was formed when the western part of Virginia refused to join the Confederacy.

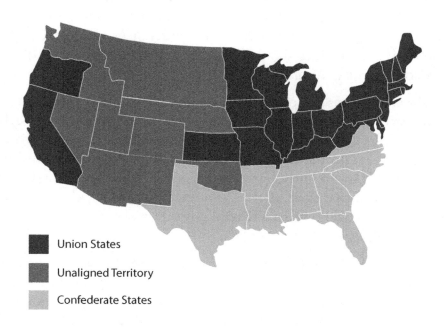

Figure 2.7. Union and Confederacy

Both sides believed the conflict would be short-lived; however, after the First Battle of Bull Run when the Union failed to rout the Confederacy, it became clear that the war would not end quickly. The Union developed the **Anaconda Plan**, which "squeezed" the Confederacy through a naval blockade and Union control of the Mississippi River. Since the South depended on international trade for much of its income, a naval blockade would have serious economic ramifications.

However, the Second Battle of Bull Run was a tactical Confederate victory, led by **General Robert E. Lee** and Stonewall Jackson. The Union army remained intact, but the loss was a heavy blow to Union morale. The Battle of Antietam was the first battle to be fought on Union soil. Union General George B. McClellan halted General Lee's invasion of Maryland, but failed to defeat Confederate forces. Undaunted, on January 1, 1863, President Lincoln decreed the end of slavery in the rebel states with the **Emancipation Proclamation**. The **Battle of Gettysburg** was a major Union victory. It was the bloodiest battle in American history up to this point; the Confederate army would not recover.

> **DID YOU KNOW?**
>
> President Lincoln later delivered the Gettysburg Address onsite, in which he framed the Civil War as a battle for human rights and equality.

Meanwhile, Union forces led by **General Ulysses S. Grant** gained control over the Mississippi River, completing the Anaconda Plan. The **Battle of Atlanta** was the final major battle of the Civil War, and the Confederacy fell. One of the final conflicts of the war, the Battle of Appomattox Court House, finally resulted in Confederate surrender at Appomattox, Virginia, on April 9, 1865, where General Lee surrendered to General Grant. The war ended shortly after.

AFTERMATH AND RECONSTRUCTION

Despite the strong leadership and vast territory of the Confederacy, a larger population, stronger industrial capacity (including weapons-making capacity), the naval blockade of Southern trade, and superior leadership resulted in Union victory. Yet bitterness over Northern victory persisted, and President Lincoln was assassinated on April 15, 1865. Post-war **Reconstruction** would continue without his leadership.

Before his death, Lincoln had crafted the **Ten Percent Plan**: if ten percent of a Southern state's population swore allegiance to the Union, that state would be readmitted. However Lincoln's vice president, Andrew Johnson, enforced Reconstruction weakly and the white supremacist **Ku Klux Klan** emerged to intimidate and kill black people in the South; likewise, states enacted the oppressive **Black Codes** to limit the rights of African Americans.

> **DID YOU KNOW?**
>
> Despite ratifying the amendments, Southern states instituted the Black Codes to continue oppression of freedmen, or freed African Americans, who faced ongoing violence.

As a result, Congress passed the **Civil Rights Act** in 1866, granting citizenship to African Americans and guaranteeing African American men the same rights as white men (later reaffirmed by the Fourteenth Amendment). Eventually former Confederate states also had to ratify the 1865 **Thirteenth Amendment**, which abolished slavery; the **Fourteenth Amendment**, which upheld the provisions of the

Civil Rights Act; and the **Fifteenth Amendment**, which in 1870 granted African American men the right to vote.

Conflict over how harshly to treat the South persisted in Congress and in 1867, a Republican-led Congress passed the **Reconstruction Acts**, placing former Confederate states under the control of the US Army, effectively declaring martial law. Tension and bitterness existed between many Northern authorities and Southern leaders. At the same time, Reconstruction modernized Southern education systems, tax collection, and infrastructure. The **Freedmen's Bureau** was tasked with assisting freed slaves (and poor whites) in the South.

While technically enslaved African Americans had been freed, many slaves were not aware of this; others still remained voluntarily or involuntarily on plantations. All slaves were eventually freed; however, few had education or skills. Despite the Fourteenth Amendment, the rights of African Americans were regularly violated. The **Jim Crow laws** enforced **segregation** in the South.

In 1896, the Supreme Court upheld segregation in *Plessy v. Ferguson* when a mixed-race man, Homer Plessy, was forced off a whites-only train car. When Plessy challenged the law, the Court found that segregation was indeed constitutional, holding that *separate but equal* did still ensure equality under the law. This would remain the law until *Brown v. Board of Education* in 1954.

Black leaders like **Booker T. Washington** and **W.E.B. DuBois** sought solutions. Washington believed in gradual desegregation and vocational education for African Americans, providing it at his **Tuskegee Institute**. DuBois, on the other hand, favored immediate desegregation and believed African Americans should aim for higher education and leadership positions in society. His stance was supported by the advocacy group, the **National Association for the Advancement of Colored People (NAACP)**. These differing views reflected diverse positions within and beyond the African American community over its future. Furthermore, many blacks fled the South for opportunities in the North and West, as part of a greater demographic movement known as the **Great Migration**.

Resentment over the Reconstruction Acts never truly subsided, and military control of the South finally ended with the **Compromise of 1877**, which resolved the disputed presidential election of 1876, granting Rutherford B. Hayes the presidency, and removed troops from the South.

While the Civil War raged and during the chaotic post-war Reconstruction period, settlement of the West continued. California had already grown in population due to the gold rush. In the mid-nineteenth century, **Chinese immigrants** came in large numbers to California, in search of gold but arriving to racial discrimination instead. At the same time, however, the US was opening up trade with East Asia, thanks to **clipper ships** that made journeys across the Pacific Ocean faster and easier. Earlier in 1853, **Commodore Matthew Perry** had used "gunboat diplomacy" to force trade agreements with Japan; even earlier, the United States had signed the **Treaty of Wangxia**, a trade agreement, with Qing Dynasty China.

Unlike Chinese immigrants, Americans of European descent were encouraged to settle the Frontier. The **Homestead Act of 1862** granted 160 acres of land in the West to any settler who promised to settle and work it for a number of years. Frontier life was hard, however, as the land of the Great Plains was difficult to farm. Meanwhile, ranching and herding cattle became popular and profitable. White settlers also hunted the buffalo; mass buffalo killings threatened Native American survival.

Conflict between Native American tribes and white settlers was ongoing. The United States came to an agreement with the Sioux in South Dakota, offering them land as part of the burgeoning **reservation** system. However, by the late nineteenth century, gold was discovered in the Black Hills of South Dakota on the **Great Sioux Reservation**, and the US reneged on its promise. The resulting **Sioux Wars** culminated in the 1876 **Battle of Little Big Horn** and General George Custer's famous "last stand." While the US was defeated in that battle, reinforcements would later defeat the Sioux and the reservation system continued. The spiritual **Ghost Dance Movement** united Plains tribes in the belief that whites would eventually be driven from the land. In 1890, the military forced the Sioux to cease this ritual; the outcome was a massacre at **Wounded Knee** and the death of the Sioux chief, **Sitting Bull**.

In 1887, the **Dawes Act** ended federal recognition of tribes, withdrew tribal land rights, and forced the sale of reservations—tribal land. It also dissolved Native American families. Children were sent to boarding schools, where they were forced to abandon their languages and cultures.

THE GILDED AGE AND THE SECOND INDUSTRIAL REVOLUTION

Back in the Northeast, the market economy and industry were flourishing. Following the war, the **Industrial Revolution** accelerated in the United States. The Industrial Revolution had begun with textile production in Great Britain, fueled in great part by Southern cotton. It evolved in the United States with the development of heavy industry into what would be called the **Second Industrial Revolution**.

The **Gilded Age** saw an era of rapidly growing income inequality, justified by theories like **Social Darwinism** and the **Gospel of Wealth**. These argued that the wealthy had been made rich by God and were more deserving of wealth than others. Much of this wealth was generated by heavy industry in the Second Industrial Revolution (the first being textile driven in Europe). Westward expansion required railroads; railroads required steel, and industrial production required oil: all these commodities spurred the rise of powerful companies like John D. Rockefeller's Standard Oil and Andrew Carnegie's US Steel.

The creation of **monopolies** and **trusts** helped industrial leaders consolidate their control over the entire economy; a small elite grew to hold a huge percentage of income. Monopolies let the same business leaders control the market for their own products. Business leaders in varying industries (monopolies) organized into trusts, ensuring their control over each other's industries, buying and selling from each other, and resulting in the control of the economy by a select few. These processes were made possible thanks to **vertical** and **horizontal integration** of industries. One company would dominate each step in manufacturing a good, from obtaining raw materials to shipping finished product, through vertical integration. Horizontal integration describes the process of companies acquiring their competition, monopolizing their markets. With limited governmental controls or interference in the economy, American **capitalism**—the free market system—was becoming dominated by the elite.

However, the elite were also powering industrial growth. Government corruption led only to weak restrictive legislation like the **Interstate Commerce Act** of 1887, which was to regulate the railroad industry, and the **Sherman Antitrust Act** (1890), which was intended to break up monopolies and trusts, in order to allow for a fairer marketplace; however, these measures would remain largely toothless until President Theodore Roosevelt's "trust-busting" administration in 1901.

Not only were products from the US market economy available in the United States; in order to continue to fuel economic growth, the United States needed more markets abroad. **New Imperialism** described the US approach to nineteenth and early twentieth century imperialism as practiced by the European powers. Rather than controlling territory, the US sought economic connections with countries around the world.

While the free markets and trade of the **capitalist** economy spurred national economic and industrial growth, the **working class**, comprised largely of poor European and Chinese immigrants working in factories and building infrastructure, suffered from dangerous working conditions and other abuses. As the railroads expanded westward, white farmers suffered: they lost their land to corporate interests. In addition, Mexican Americans and Native Americans were harmed and lost land as westward expansion continued with little to no regulations on land use. African Americans in the South, though freed from slavery, were also struggling under **sharecropping**, in which many worked for the same people who had enslaved them, leasing land and equipment at unreasonable rates, essentially trapped in the same conditions they had lived in before.

These harmful consequences led to the development of reform movements, social ideals, and change.

POPULISM AND THE PROGRESSIVE ERA

The **People's (Populist) Party** formed in response to corruption and industrialization injurious to farmers (later, it would also support reform in favor of the working class, women, and children). Westward expansion destroyed farmland, pushing small farmers off their land and into debt. Small farmers were also unable to keep up with mechanized farming. Groups like the **National Grange** advocated for farmers. More extreme groups like **Las Gorras Blancas** disrupted the construction of railroads altogether in efforts to protect land from corporate interests.

Farmers were also concerned about fiscal policy. In order to reduce their debt, they believed that a **silver standard** would inflate crop prices by putting more money into national circulation, and formed the **Greenback-Labor Party**. The 1890 **Sherman Silver Purchase Act** allowed Treasury notes to be backed in both gold and silver. However, continuing economic troubles led to the **Panic of 1893**, and the act was repealed.

Meanwhile, the **Colored Farmers' Alliance** formed to support sharecroppers and other African American farmers in the South. Jim Crow laws remained in place in much of the South, reaffirmed by the Supreme Court case *Plessy v. Ferguson*. The NAACP was formed to advocate for African Americans nationwide and still functions today.

At the same time, the **labor movement** emerged to support mistreated industrial workers in urban areas. **Samuel Gompers** led the **American Federation of Labor (AFL)**, using **strikes** and **collective bargaining** to gain protections for industrial workers. The **Knights of Labor** further empowered workers by integrating unskilled workers into actions. The activist **Mother Jones** revolutionized labor by including women, children, and African Americans into labor actions.

Poor conditions led to philosophies of reform. Many workers were inspired by **socialism**, the philosophy developed in Europe that the workers should own the means of production and that wealth should be distributed equally, taking into account strong economic planning. Other radical movements included **utopianism**, whose adherents conceptualized establishing utopian settlements with egalitarian societies. More modern philosophies included the **Social Gospel**, the notion that it was society's obligation to ensure better treatment for workers and immigrants. With the continual rise of the **middle class**, women took a more active role in advocating for the poor and for themselves. Women activists also aligned with labor and the emerging **Progressive Movement**.

With the Progressive **Theodore Roosevelt**'s ascension to the presidency in 1901 following President William McKinley's assassination, the Progressive Era reached its apex. The *trust-buster* Roosevelt enforced the Sherman Antitrust Act and prosecuted the powerful **Northern Securities** railroad monopoly under the Interstate Commerce Act, breaking up trusts and creating a fairer market. He led government involvement in negotiations between unions and industrial powers, culminating in what was known as a *square deal* for fairer treatment of workers. The Progressive Era also saw a series of acts to protect workers, health, farmers, and children under Presidents Roosevelt and Taft.

Roosevelt also continued overseas expansion following McKinley's **Spanish-American War** (1898–1901), in which the US gained control over Spanish territory in the Caribbean, Asia, and the South Pacific.

The Spanish-American War had been the first time the United States had engaged in overseas military occupation and conquest beyond North America, contrary to George Washington's recommendations in his Farewell Address.

During this period, the US annexed Hawaii, Guam, Puerto Rico, and took over the Panama Canal Zone; Cuba became a US protectorate; and the US annexed the Philippines, which would fight an ongoing guerrilla war for independence.

Spanish abuses in Cuba had concerned Americans; however, many events were exaggerated in the media. This sensational **yellow journalism** aroused popular interest in intervention in Cuba. The discovery of a diplomatically embarrassing letter from the Spanish minister de Lôme, along with the mysterious explosion of the battleship USS *Maine* in Havana, spurred the US into action.

Many Americans did not support intervention, however. According to the **Teller Amendment**, Cuba would revert to independence following the war. The US signed a peace treaty with Spain in 1898. As a result, it controlled Puerto Rico and Guam. Despite having promised independence to the Philippines, McKinley elected to keep it; furthermore, under the **Platt Amendment**, the United States effectively took over Cuba despite previous promises.

The **Roosevelt Corollary** to the Monroe Doctrine, which promised US intervention in Latin America in case of European intervention there, essentially gave the US total dominance over Latin America. Under the **Hay-Pauncefote Treaty**, Great Britain relinquished its claims to the Panama Canal Zone to the US. This **new imperialism** expanded US markets and increased US presence and prestige on the global stage.

SAMPLE QUESTIONS

16) **Which of the following is true about the roots of the Civil War?**

   A.   Disagreement over the institution of slavery precipitated the Nullification Crisis, an early example of Southern discontent with the federal government.

   B.   High numbers of immigrants moving to the North in the early nineteenth century represented a threat to the smaller South, which wanted to maintain control over the slaves.

   C.   Lincoln and Douglas provoked anti-slavery sentiment in their debates around the country, bringing attention to a previously uncontested issue.

   D.   The Missouri Compromise, the Compromise of 1850, and the Kansas-Nebraska Act reflected dissent over the future of the country—whether slavery should be extended as the United States grew.

Answer:

   D.   **Correct.** These pieces of legislation represent ongoing efforts to bridge the gap between differences in views over slavery in determining the future of the country.

17) **How did the Dawes Act impact Native Americans in the West?**

    A.   It forced them to move from their ancestral lands to what is today Oklahoma.

    B.   It revoked tribal rights to land and federal recognition of tribes, forcing assimilation.

    C.   It granted them land on reservations: for example, the Sioux received deeds to the Great Sioux Reservation in the Black Hills of South Dakota.

    D.   It provided 160 acres of land to any settler willing to farm land on the Great Plains for at least five years, threatening Native American rights to land.

    Answer:

    B.   **Correct.** The punitive Dawes Act forced assimilation by revoking federal recognition of tribes, taking lands allotted to tribes and dissolving reservations, and forcing children into assimilationist schools (thereby dividing families).

18) **How was a small elite of wealthy businesspersons able to dominate the economy during the Gilded Age?**

    A.   The Sherman Antitrust Act put a few expert business leaders in charge of economic policy.

    B.   Monopolies and trusts, developed through horizontal and vertical integration, ensured that the same business leaders controlled the same markets.

    C.   Industrialization was encouraging the United States to shift to a planned economy in keeping with philosophical changes in Europe.

    D.   The silver standard allowed specific businesspeople holding large silver reserves to dominate the market.

    Answer:

    B.   **Correct.** Horizontal and vertical integration of industries allowed the same companies—and people—to control industries, or create monopolies. Those elites who monopolized specific markets organized trusts so that one group controlled entire sectors of the economy.

19) **How did the Spanish-American War change perceptions of the United States?**

    A.   It was clear to Europe and Latin America that the United States had military and territorial, in addition to economic, aspirations as an imperial power.

    B.   The United States had begun to prove itself as a military power on the global stage, with strong naval capabilities.

    C.   It was clear that nationalism was strong among the American people.

    D.   all of the above

Answer:

D.   Correct. All of the above answer choices satisfy the question.

20) **How did the Progressive Movement change the United States during the Second Industrial Revolution?**

A.   Trade unions fought for workers' rights and safety; the Social Gospel, an early philosophy of charity and philanthropy, developed to support the poor and urban disadvantaged.

B.   The Seneca Falls Convention drew attention to the question of women's suffrage.

C.   Progressives argued to extend rights and protections to Native Americans, particularly those displaced by settlement on the Great Plains.

D.   The Supreme Court ruled segregation unconstitutional in *Plessy v. Ferguson.*

Answer:

A.   Correct. Unions improved conditions for industrial workers; the Social Gospel imparted a sense of social responsibility that manifested in laws and regulations protecting the rights and safety of workers, farmers, the poor, and others.

The United States Becomes a Global Power

Socioeconomic Change and World War I

Social change led by the Progressives in the early twentieth century resulted in better conditions for workers, increased attention toward child labor, and calls for more livable cities.

The Roosevelt administration focused its attention on economic change at the corporate level. The **Sherman Antitrust Act**, despite its intended purpose—to prosecute and dissolve large trusts and create a fairer market place—had actually been used against unions and farmers' alliances. Under Roosevelt, the Act was used to prosecute enormous trusts like the **Northern Securities Company**, which controlled much of the railroad industry, and **Standard Oil**. Actions like this earned Roosevelt his reputation as a trust-buster.

Continuing economic instability also triggered top-down reform. Banks restricting credit and overspeculating on the value of land and interests, coupled with a conservative gold standard, led to the **Panic of 1907**. To stabilize the economy and protect the banking system, Congress passed the **Federal Reserve Act** in 1913. Federal Reserve banks were established to cover twelve regions of the country; commercial banks had to take part in the system, allowing "the Fed" to control interest rates and avoid a similar crisis.

During the Progressive Era, while the United States became increasingly prosperous and stable, Europe was becoming increasingly unstable. Americans were divided over how to respond. Following the Spanish-American War, debate had arisen within the US between **interventionism** and **isolationism**—whether the US should intervene in international matters or not. Interventionists believed in spreading US-style democracy, while isolationists believed in focusing on development at home. This debate became more pronounced with the outbreak of World War I in Europe.

Inflammatory events like German **submarine warfare** (U-boats) in the Atlantic Ocean, the sinking of the *Lusitania*, which resulted in many American civilian deaths, the embarrassing **Zimmerman Telegram** (in which Germany promised to help Mexico in an attack on the US), and growing American **nationalism**, or pride in and identification with one's country, triggered US intervention. The US declared war in 1917. With victory in 1918, the US had proven itself a superior military and industrial power. Interventionist **President Woodrow Wilson** played an important role in negotiating the peace; his **Fourteen Points** laid out an idealistic international vision, including an international security organization. However, European powers negotiated and won the harsh **Treaty of Versailles**, which placed the blame for the war entirely on Germany and demanded crippling **reparations** from it, one contributing factor to **World War II** later in the twentieth century. The **League of Nations**, a collective security organization, was formed, but a divided US Congress refused to ratify the Treaty, so the US did not join it. Consequently, the League was weak and largely ineffective.

Divisions between interventionists and isolationists continued. Following the Japanese invasion of Manchuria in 1932, the **Stimson Doctrine** determined US neutrality in Asia. Congress also passed the **Neutrality Acts** of the 1930s in face of conflict in Asia and ongoing tensions in Europe.

Fear of homegrown radicals—particularly communists and anarchists—and xenophobia against immigrants led to the **Red Scare** in 1919 and a series of anti-immigration laws. Congress limited immigration specifically from Asia, Eastern Europe, and Southern Europe with the racist **Emergency Quota Act** of 1921 and **National Origins Act** of 1924.

The ongoing Great Migration of African Americans to the North led to differing views on black empowerment. Leaders like **Marcus Garvey** believed in self-sufficiency for blacks, who were settling in urban areas and facing racial discrimination and isolation. Garvey's **United Negro Improvement Association** would go on to inspire movements like the Black Panthers and the Nation of Islam; however, those radical philosophies of separation were at odds with the NAACP, which believed in integration. Tensions increased with 1919 race riots. In the South, the Ku Klux

Klan was growing in power, and blacks faced intimidation, violence, and death; **lynchings**, in which African Americans were kidnapped and killed, sometimes publicly, occurred frequently.

Despite race riots and discrimination in northern cities, African American culture did flourish and become an integral part of growing American popular culture. The **Harlem Renaissance**, the development and popularity of African American-dominated music (especially **jazz**), literature, and art, was extremely popular nationwide and contributed to the development of American pop culture.

Early technology like radio, motion pictures, and automobiles—products available to the middle class through credit—emerged in the 1920s, changing the US middle class and encouraging a culture of consumption. Furthermore, the women's rights movement was empowered by the heightened visibility of women in the public sphere; the **Nineteenth Amendment**, giving all women the right to vote, was ratified in 1920. However, the **Roaring Twenties**, a seemingly trouble-free period of isolation from chaotic world events, would come to an end.

GREAT DEPRESSION

Following WWI, the United States had experienced an era of consumerism and corruption. The government sponsored **laissez-faire** policies and supported **manufacturing**, flooding markets with cheap consumer goods. Union membership suffered; so did farmers, due to falling crop prices. While mass production helped the emerging middle class afford more consumer goods and improve their living standards, many families resorted to **credit** to fuel consumer spending. These risky consumer loans, **overspeculation** on crops and the value of farmland, and weak banking protections helped bring about the **Great Depression**, commonly dated from October 29, 1929, or *Black Tuesday*, when the stock market collapsed. During the same time period, a major drought occurred in the Great Plains, affecting farmers throughout the region. Millions of Americans faced unemployment and poverty.

Speculation, or margin buying, meant that speculators borrowed money to buy stock, selling it as soon as its price rose. However, since the price of stocks fluctuated, when buyers lost confidence in the market and began selling their shares, the value of stocks fell. Borrowers could not repay their loans; as a result, banks failed.

Following weak responses by the Hoover administration, **Franklin Delano Roosevelt** was elected to the presidency in 1932. FDR offered Americans a *New Deal*: a plan to bring the country out of the Depression. During the *First Hundred Days* of FDR's administration, a series of emergency acts (known as an *alphabet soup* of acts due to their many acronyms) was passed for the immediate repair of the banking system. The **Glass-Steagal Act** established the **Federal Deposit Insurance Corporation (FDIC)** to insure customer deposits in the wake of bank failures. The **Securities and Exchange Commission (SEC)** was established later to monitor stock trading and punish violators of the law. The **Agricultural Adjustment Act (AAA)** subsidized farmers to reduce production, benefitting them by raising the prices of commodities. The **Home Owners Loan Corporation (HOLC)** refinanced mortgages to protect homeowners from losing their homes, and the **Federal Housing Administration (FHA)** was created for the long term to insure low-cost mortgages.

Figure 2.8. Soup Kitchen During the Great Depression

The **Tennessee Valley Authority (TVA),** was the first large-scale attempt at regional public planning; despite being part of the First Hundred Days, it was a long-term project. While intended to create jobs and bring electricity to the impoverished, rural inhabitants of the Tennessee Valley area, one of its true objectives was to accurately measure the cost of electric power, which had been supplied by private companies. The TVA was the first public power company and still operates today.

FDR did not only address economic issues; a number of acts provided relief to the poor and unemployed. The federal government allotted aid to states to be distributed directly to the poor through the **Federal Emergency Relief Act**. The federal government distributed funding to states through the **Public Works Administration (PWA)** for the purpose of developing infrastructure and to provide construction jobs for the unemployed. Likewise, the **Civilian Conservation Corps (CCC)** offered employment in environmental conservation and management projects. Later, during the **Second New Deal**, the **Works Progress Administration (WPA)** was established. The WPA was a long-term project that generated construction jobs on national infrastructure projects. It also employed writers and artists through the **Federal Writers' Project** and the **Federal Art Project**.

The New Deal addressed labor issues as well. The **Wagner Act** ensured the right to unionize and established the **National Labor Relations Board (NLRB)**. Strengthening unions guaranteed collective bargaining rights and protected workers.

FDR was a Democrat in the Progressive tradition; the Progressive legacy of social improvement was apparent throughout the New Deal and his administration. The New Deal and its positive impact on the poor, the working class, unions, and immigrants led these groups to support the Democratic Party.

INTERNATIONAL AFFAIRS AND WORLD WAR II

The entire world suffered from the Great Depression, and Europe became increasingly unstable. With the rise of the extremist Nazi Party in Germany, the Nazi leader Adolf Hitler led German takeovers of several European countries and threatened US allies, bombing Britain. However, the United States, weakened by the Great Depression and bound by the Neutrality Acts, remained militarily uncommitted in the war. However, the Neutrality Act of 1939 allowed cash-and-carry arms sales to combat participants; in this way, the United States could support its allies (namely, Great Britain).

FDR was increasingly concerned about the rise of fascism in Europe, seeing it as a global threat. To ally with and support Great Britain without technically declaring war on Germany, FDR convinced Congress to enact the **Lend-Lease Act**, directly supplying Britain with military aid, in place of cash-and-carry. In response to the nonaggression pact signed by Hitler and Stalin, FDR and the British Prime Minister **Winston Churchill** signed the **Atlantic Charter**, which laid out the anti-fascist agenda of free trade and self-determination. To garner domestic support, FDR spoke publicly about the **Four Freedoms**: freedom of speech, freedom of religion, freedom from want, and freedom from fear.

However, after the Japanese attack on **Pearl Harbor** on December 7, 1941, the US entered the war. Despite being attacked by Japan (a German ally), the United States focused first on the European theater. The Allied powers—the US, Great Britain, and the Soviet Union—agreed that Hitler was the primary global threat. The United States focused on eliminating the Nazi threat in the air and at sea, destroying Nazi U-boats (submarines) in the Atlantic. The US also engaged Germany in North Africa, defeating its troops to approach fascist Italy from the Mediterranean. On June 6, 1944, or **D-Day**, the US led the invasion of German-controlled Europe at Normandy. After months of fighting, following the exhausting **Battle of the Bulge** when the Allies faced fierce German resistance, the Allies entered Germany and ended the war in Europe.

The United States was then able to focus more effectively on the war in the Pacific. The United States had broken Japanese code, yet the **Navajo Code Talkers**, using the Navajo language, made it impossible for Japan to crack US code. The US strategy of **island hopping** allowed it to take control of Japanese-held Pacific islands, proceeding closer to Japan itself despite **kamikaze** attacks on US ships, in which Japanese fighter pilots intentionally crashed their planes into US ships. President **Harry Truman** had taken power following FDR's death in 1945. Rather than force a US invasion of Japan, which would have resulted in massive casualties, he authorized the bombing of **Hiroshima** and **Nagasaki** in Japan, the only times that **nuclear weapons** have been used in conflict. The war ended with Japanese surrender on September 2, 1945.

The **United Nations** was formed in the wake of the Second World War, modeled after the failed League of Nations. Unlike the League, however, it included a **Security Council** of major world powers, which could intervene militarily in unstable global situations. With most of Europe destroyed, the US and the Soviet Union emerged as the two global **superpowers**.

In 1945, Stalin, Churchill, and Roosevelt had met at the **Yalta Conference** to determine the future of Europe. The Allies had agreed on free elections in European countries. However, following the war the USSR occupied Eastern Europe, preventing free elections. The United States saw this as a betrayal of the agreement at Yalta. Furthermore, while the US-led **Marshall Plan** began rebuilding Europe, the USSR consolidated its presence and power in Eastern European countries, forcing them to reject Marshall aid. This division would destroy the alliance between the Soviets and the West, leading to the **Cold War** between the two superpowers and the emergence of a **bipolar world**.

> **DID YOU KNOW?**
>
> Japanese-Americans faced discrimination at home due to their ethnicity. Forced into internment camps, Japanese-Americans challenged this violation of their rights in *Korematsu v. US*; however, the Supreme Court ruled in favor of the government.

COLD WAR AT HOME AND ABROAD

With the collapse of the relationship between the USSR and the US, fear of **communism** grew. Accusations of communist sympathies against public figures ran rampant during the **McCarthy era** in the 1950s, reflecting domestic anxieties.

The **Truman Doctrine** stated that the US would support any country threatened by authoritarianism (communism). This policy lead to the **Korean War** (1950 – 1953), a conflict between the US and Soviet- and Chinese-backed North Korean forces, which ended in a stalemate. The policy of **containment**, to contain Soviet (communist) expansion, defined US foreign policy. According to **domino theory**, once one country fell to communism, others would quickly follow. Other incidents included the **Bay of Pigs** invasion in Cuba (1961), a failed effort to topple the communist government of Fidel Castro, and the **Cuban Missile Crisis** (1962), when Soviet missiles were discovered in Cuba and military crisis was narrowly averted, both under the administration of the popular President **John F. Kennedy**.

Meanwhile, in Southeast Asia, communist forces in North Vietnam were gaining power. Congress never formally declared war in Vietnam but gave the president authority to intervene militarily there through the **Gulf of Tonkin Resolution** (1964). However, this protracted conflict—the **Vietnam War**—also led to widespread domestic social unrest, which only increased with US deaths there, especially after the Vietnamese **Tet Offensive** (1968). The US ultimately withdrew from Vietnam. North Vietnamese forces, led by **Ho Chi Minh**, took over the entire country.

SAMPLE QUESTIONS

21) **Which of the following precipitated US entry into the First World War?**

   A.   the sinking of the *Lusitania*

   B.   nationalism stirred up by the Zimmerman telegram

   C.   the threat of German U-boats in the Atlantic

   D.   all of the above

   Answer:

   D.   Correct. All of the above events together precipitated US entry into the First World War.

22) **How did the United States change in the 1920s?**

   A.   The Great Migration ceased.

   B.   African American culture became increasingly influential.

   C.   The Great Depression caused high unemployment.

   D.   Thanks to the New Deal, millions of Americans found jobs.

   Answer:

   B.   Correct. The Harlem Renaissance is one example of the emergence of African American culture in the public sphere; as US popular culture developed, African American contributions influenced it.

23) **What was the purpose of the United Nations Security Council?**

   A.   to provide a means for international military intervention in case of conflict that could threaten global safety, in order to avoid another world war

   B.   to provide a forum for the superpowers to maintain a dialogue

   C.   to provide a means for countries to counter the power of the US and USSR in an effort to limit the reach of the superpowers

   D.   to develop a plan to rebuild Europe and Japan

Answer:

A.   Correct. The Security Council was (and is) able to militarily intervene in cases of armed conflict that could pose a global threat.

24) **How did the New Deal repair the damage of the Great Depression and help the United States rebuild?**

A.   Immediate economic reforms stabilized the economy during the First Hundred Days; later, longer-term public works programs provided jobs to relieve unemployment and develop infrastructure.

B.   Social programs initiated during the First Hundred Days provided jobs for Americans; measures to protect homeowners, landholders, and bank deposits followed to guarantee financial security.

C.   Programs like the Tennessee Valley Authority helped the government determine proper pricing and institute price controls for important public goods.

D.   FDR proposed supporting banks and big business with federal money in order to reinvigorate the market by limiting government intervention.

Answer:

A.   Correct. FDR focused on immediate economic stabilization upon taking office, then attacked poverty and unemployment on a sustainable basis.

25) **Why did the former allies, the United States and the Soviet Union, turn against each other following the end of the Second World War?**

A.   Stalin felt that the Marshall Plan should have been extended to the Soviet Union.

B.   Because of the fear of communism in the United States, the US had considered invading the USSR following the occupation of Nazi Germany.

C.   Despite assurances to the contrary, the USSR occupied Eastern European countries, preventing free elections in those countries.

D.   The Soviet Union was concerned that the United States would use the nuclear bomb again.

Answer:

C.   Correct. Stalin's refusal to permit free elections in the countries of Eastern Europe was considered a betrayal of the agreement reached at Yalta, and a major reason for the collapse of the US-Soviet relationship.

POSTWAR AND CONTEMPORARY UNITED STATES

CIVIL RIGHTS AND SOCIAL CHANGE

During the 1960s, the US experienced social and political change, starting with the election of the young and charismatic John F. Kennedy to the presidency. Later, President **Lyndon B. Johnson**'s administration saw the passage of liberal legislation in support of the poor and of civil rights. The **Civil Rights Movement**, led by activists like the **Rev. Dr. Martin Luther King, Jr.** and **Malcolm X**, fought for African American rights in the South, including the abolition of segregation, and also for better living standards for Blacks in northern cities.

Civil rights came to the forefront with the 1954 Supreme Court case *Brown v. Board of Education*, when the Warren Court (so-called after Chief Justice Earl Warren) found segregation unconstitutional, overturning its decision in *Plessy v. Ferguson*. *Brown* took place shortly after the desegregation of the armed forces, and public support for civil rights and racial equality was growing.

The **Southern Christian Leadership Conference (SCLC)** and Dr. King believed in civil disobedience, non-violent protest. In Montgomery, Alabama, **Rosa Parks**, an African American woman, was arrested for refusing to give up her seat to a white man on a bus. Buses were segregated at the time, and leaders including Dr. King organized the successful **Montgomery Bus Boycott** to challenge segregation. Building on their success, civil rights activists, now including the **Student Nonviolent Coordinating Committee (SNCC)**, led peaceful protests, sit-ins, and boycotts against segregation at lunch counters, in stores, at public pools, and other public places.

The movement grew to include voter registration campaigns that included students and other activists (both black and white) from around the country—the **Freedom Riders**, so-called because they rode buses from around the country to join the movement in the South. The movement gained visibility as non-violent protesters at government and public facilities and on university campuses faced violence from the police and state authorities, including attacks by water cannons and police dogs.

The Civil Rights Movement became a major national issue. Civil rights workers organized the **March on Washington** in 1963, when Dr. King delivered his famous *I Have a Dream* speech. Widespread public support for civil rights legislation was impossible for the government to ignore. In 1964, Congress passed the **Civil Rights Act**, which outlawed segregation.

However, African Americans' voting rights were still not sufficiently protected. According to the Fifteenth and Nineteenth Amendments, all African Americans—men and women—had the right to vote, but many Southern states restricted voting with literacy tests and poll taxes, which disproportionately affected African Americans. Dr. King and civil rights workers organized a march from Selma to Montgomery, Alabama, to draw attention to this issue; however it ended in violence as marchers were attacked by police. In 1965, led by President Lyndon B. Johnson, Congress passed the **Voting Rights Act**, which forbade restrictions impeding the ability of African Americans to vote, including literacy tests. Separately, the **Twenty-Fourth Amendment** made poll taxes unconstitutional.

Figure 2.9. March on Washington

Meanwhile, **Malcolm X** was an outspoken proponent of **black empowerment**, particularly for African Americans in urban areas. Unlike Martin Luther King, Jr., who believed in integration, Malcolm X and other activists, including groups like the **Black Panthers**, believed that African Americans should focus on strengthening their own communities rather than advocating for integration and legislative change.

The Civil Rights Movement extended beyond the Deep South. **Cesar Chavez** founded the **United Farm Workers (UFW)**, which organized Hispanic and migrant farm workers in California and the Southwest to advocate for unionizing and collective bargaining. Farm workers were underpaid and faced racial discrimination. The UFW used boycotts and non-violent tactics similar to those used by civil rights activists in the South; Cesar Chavez also used hunger strikes to raise awareness of the problems faced by farm workers.

DID YOU KNOW?

Today, some states have instituted voter identification laws similar to literacy tests and poll taxes, which disproportionately affect minorities.

The Civil Rights Movement also included **feminist** activists who fought for fairer treatment of women in the workplace and for women's reproductive rights. The **National Organization for Women** and feminist leaders like **Gloria Steinem** led the movement for equal pay for women in the workplace. The landmark case of *Roe v. Wade* struck down federal restrictions on abortion.

The **American Indian Movement (AIM)** brought attention to injustices and discrimination suffered by Native Americans nationwide. Ultimately it was able to achieve more tribal autonomy and address problems facing Native American communities throughout the United States.

In New York City in 1969, the **Stonewall riots** occurred in response to police repression of the gay community. These riots and subsequent organized activism are considered the beginning of the LGBT rights movement.

Johnson launched a **War on Poverty**, passing reform legislation to support the poor. The **Medicare Act** provided medical care to elderly Americans; the creation of the **Department of Housing and Urban Development** increased the federal role in housing and urban issues. Johnson's **Head Start** program provisded early intervention for disadvantaged children before elementary school (and still does today); the **Elementary and Secondary Education Act** increased funding for primary and secondary education. Additionally, the **Immigration Act of 1965** overturned the provisions of the Emergency Quota Act, ending the racist limitations on immigrants to the US.

At the same time, LBJ's overseas agenda was increasingly unpopular. Adhering to containment and domino theory, Johnson drew the United States deeper into conflict in Southeast Asia. The **Vietnam War** was extremely unpopular in the US due to high casualties, the draft (mandatory military service for young men) and what seemed to many to be the purposelessness of the war. Student activists engaged in widespread protest. The emergence of a youth **counterculture** added to a sense of rebellion among Americans, usurping government authority and challenging traditional values.

THE RISE OF CONSERVATISM

Radical social change in the 1960s, coupled with the toll of the Vietnam War on the American public, led to backlash against liberalism. Social and political **conservatism** arose as a response to the increased role of government in public life, high rates of government spending, and challenges to traditional social norms. The conservative **Richard Nixon** became president in 1970.

During Nixon's administration, the conflict in Vietnam ended and a diplomatic relationship with China began. Nixon also oversaw economic reforms—he lifted the gold standard in an effort to stop **stagflation**, a phenomenon when both unemployment and inflation are high at the same time. Ending the gold standard reduced the value of the dollar in relation to other global currencies, and foreign investment in the United States increased. However, the Nixon administration also suffered from corruption. A burglary at the Democratic National Headquarters, based at the Watergate Hotel, was connected to the Oval Office. The **Watergate scandal** eventually forced Nixon to resign, further destroying many Americans' faith in their government.

During the 1970s, the economy suffered due to US involvement in the Middle East. US support for Israel in the Six Day War and 1973 Yom Kippur War caused the Arab-dominated **OPEC** (the Organization of Petroleum Exporting Countries) to boycott the US. As a result, oil prices skyrocketed. In the 1979 Iranian Revolution and **hostage crisis**, when staff at the US embassy in Tehran were taken hostage by anti-American activists, the economy suffered from another oil shock. While President Jimmy Carter had been able to negotiate peace between Israel and Egypt in the **Camp David Accords**, he was widely perceived as ineffective. Carter lost the presidency in 1980 to the conservative Republican **Ronald Reagan**.

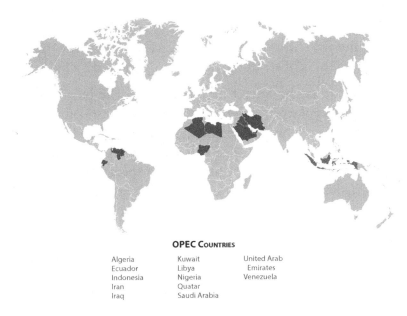

OPEC COUNTRIES

Algeria	Kuwait	United Arab
Ecuador	Libya	Emirates
Indonesia	Nigeria	Venezuela
Iran	Quatar	
Iraq	Saudi Arabia	

Figure 2.10. OPEC

Reagan championed domestic tax cuts and an aggressive foreign policy against the Soviet Union. The Reagan Revolution revamped the economic system, cutting taxes and government spending. According to supply-side economics (popularly known as *Reaganomics* or *trickle-down economics*), cutting taxes on the wealthy and providing investment incentives would cause wealth to "trickle down" to the middle and working classes and the poor. However, tax cuts forced Congress to cut or eliminate social programs that benefitted millions of those same Americans. Later, the **Tax Reform Act** of 1986 ended progressive income taxation.

Despite promises to lower government spending, the Reagan administration invested heavily in the military in an **arms race** with the Soviet Union. The Reagan administration also funded advanced military technology to intimidate the Soviets, despite having signed the **Strategic Arms Limitation Treaties (SALT I and II)** limiting nuclear weapons and other strategic armaments in the 1970s. Ultimately, the US would outspend the USSR militarily, a precipitating factor in the fall of the USSR.

Conservative values became publicly popular. Since the Civil Rights Movement, many Southern Democrats switched loyalties to the Republican Party. At the same time, the Democrats gained the support of African Americans and other minority groups who benefitted from civil rights and liberal legislation. During the Reagan era, conservative Republicans espoused a return to "traditional" values. **Christian fundamentalism** became popular, particularly among white conservatives. Groups like **Focus on the Family** lobbied against civil rights reform for women and advocated for traditional, two-parent, heterosexual families.

THE END OF THE COLD WAR AND GLOBALIZATION

The administration of **George H. W. Bush** signed the Strategic Arms Reduction Treaty (**START**) with the Soviet Union in 1991, shortly before the dissolution of the USSR. It would enter into force in 1994 between the US and the Russian Federation to limit the large arsenals of strategic weapons possessed by both countries.

With the collapse of the Soviet Union in 1991, the balance of international power changed. The bipolar world became a unipolar world, and the United States was the sole superpower. The first major crisis occurred in the Middle East when Iraq, led by **Saddam Hussein**, invaded oil-rich Kuwait. The US intervened, with international support. The resulting **Gulf War**, or **Operation Desert Storm** (1991)—cemented the status of the US as the world's sole superpower; Saddam's forces were driven from Kuwait, and Iraq was restrained by sanctions and no-fly zones.

With the election of President **Bill Clinton** in 1992, the US took an active international role, helping broker peace deals in the former Yugoslavia, Northern Ireland, and the Middle East. Clinton's election also indicated a more liberal era in American society: while conservative elements remained, changing attitudes toward minorities in the public sphere and increased global communication (especially with the advent of the internet) were a hallmark of the 1990s.

As part of **globalization**, the facilitation of global commerce and communication, the Clinton administration prioritized free trade. The United States signed the **North American Free Trade Agreement (NAFTA)** with Mexico and Canada, removing trade restrictions throughout North America. The Clinton administration also eased financial restrictions in the United States. These changes were controversial: many American jobs went overseas, especially manufacturing jobs, where labor was cheaper. Furthermore, globalization facilitated the movement of people. **Immigration reform** would be a major issue into the twenty-first century.

Clinton faced dissent in the mid-1990s with a conservative resurgence. A movement of young conservatives elected to Congress in 1994 promised a **Contract with America**, a conservative platform promising a return to lower taxes and traditional values. Clinton also came under fire for personal scandals. Despite these controversies and political division, society became increasingly liberal. Technology like the **internet** facilitated national and global communication, media, and business; minority groups like the LGBT community engaged in more advocacy; and environmental issues became more important to the public.

THE TWENTY-FIRST CENTURY

By the end of the twentieth century, the United States had established itself as the dominant global economic, military, and political power. The US dominated global trade: American corporations established themselves globally, taking advantage of free trade to exploit cheap labor pools and less restrictive manufacturing environments (at the expense of American workers). American culture was widely popular: since the early twentieth century, American pop culture like music, movies, television shows, and fashion was enjoyed worldwide.

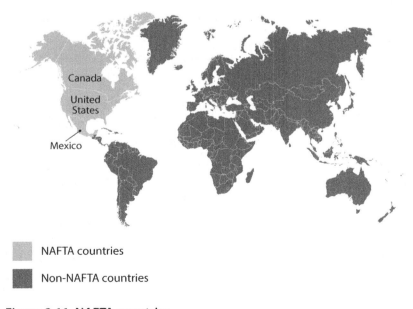

Figure 2.11. NAFTA countries

However, globalization also facilitated global conflict. The United States had been relatively untouched by large-scale terrorist attacks. That changed on **September 11, 2001**, when the terrorist group **al Qaeda** hijacked airplanes, attacking New York and Washington, DC, in the largest attack on US soil since the Japanese bombing of Pearl Harbor. The 9/11 attacks triggered an aggressive military and foreign policy under the administration of President **George W. Bush**, who declared a *War on Terror*, an open-ended global conflict against terror organizations and their supporters.

Following the attacks, the US struck suspected al Qaeda bases in Afghanistan, beginning the **Afghanistan War**, during which time the US occupied the country. Suspected terrorist fighters captured there and elsewhere during the War on Terror were held in a prison in **Guantanamo Bay**, Cuba, which was controversial because it did not initially offer any protections afforded to prisoners of war under the Geneva Conventions.

President Bush believed in the doctrine of **preemption**, that if the US was aware of a threat, it should preemptively attack the source of that threat. In 2003, the US attacked Iraq, believing that Iraq held **weapons of mass destruction** that could threaten the United States. This assumption was later revealed to be false; however, the **Iraq War** deposed Saddam Hussein and led to a long-term occupation of the country as well as destabilization and violence in Iraq.

At home, Congress passed the **USA Patriot Act** to respond to fears of more terrorist attacks on US soil; this legislation gave the federal government unprecedented—and, some argued, unconstitutional—powers of surveillance over the American public.

Despite the tense climate, social liberalization continued in the US. Following the Bush administration, during which tax cuts and heavy reliance on credit helped push the country into the **Great Recession**, the first African American president, **Barack Obama**, was elected in 2008. Under his presidency, the US emerged from the recession, ended its occupations of Iraq and Afghanistan, passed the Affordable Care Act, which reformed the healthcare system, and legalized same-sex marriage. The Obama administration also oversaw the passage of consumer protection acts, increased support for students, and safety nets for homeowners.

In 2016, the celebrity real estate developer **Donald Trump** won the presidency in an intensely contested election against **Hillary Clinton**, former senator, Obama's secretary of state, and the first female Democratic nominee for president. Economic malaise, racial tensions, urbanization, and other issues are thought to be contributing to national division. Some strongly support Trump, whose isolationist policies include withdrawing from the international Paris Agreement to combat climate change, banning citizens of some Muslim-majority countries from the US, and cutting involvement in NATO. Others vehemently disagree with his positions, accuse him of corruption, and are suspicious of the authenticity of his election, fearing it was unfairly influenced by the Russian Federation.

SAMPLE QUESTIONS

26) **Why did the Civil Rights Movement continue to push for legislative change even after the passage of the 1964 Civil Rights Act?**

A.   While the Civil Rights Act provided legal protections to African Americans and other groups, many believed it did not go far enough as it did not outlaw segregation.

B.   Leaders like Malcolm X believed further legislative reform would ensure better living conditions for blacks in cities.

C.   Civil rights leaders wanted legislation to punish white authorities in the South that had oppressed African Americans.

D.   Legal restrictions like literacy tests, poll taxes, and voter registration issues inhibited African Americans from exercising their right to vote, especially in the South.

Answer:

D.   Correct. Despite the end to legal segregation, discrimination was deeply entrenched, and laws still existed to prevent African Americans from voting. Civil rights activists worked to ensure the passage of the Voting Rights Act in 1965.

27) **Which of the following best describes liberalism under LBJ?**

A.   Liberalism was the philosophy that the government should be deeply involved in improving society at home, and work on fighting communism abroad.

B.   According to liberalism, the US should devote its resources to improving life at home for the disadvantaged, but refrain from direct intervention in international conflict.

C.   Liberals believed in moderate social programs, but that spending should be limited.

D.   Liberalism frowns upon conflict intervention, as shown by the mass demonstrations against the Vietnam War in the 1960s.

Answer:

A.   Correct. LBJ believed in forming a Great Society and launched government programs to support the disadvantaged; he also waged an unsuccessful war against communism in Southeast Asia.

28) **Which of the following best describes globalization?**

A.   the free movement of goods and services across borders

B.   easier communication worldwide thanks to technology like the internet

C.   facilitated movement of persons from one country to another

D.   all of the above

Answer:

D. **Correct.** Globalization is a multifaceted phenomenon that takes into account all the factors listed above.

29) **How did Reagan's economic policies affect working class and poor Americans?**

A. They had little effect on these classes because the United States has a free market economy.

B. They increased taxes by eliminating the progressive income tax and cut social programs needed by many disadvantaged people.

C. They benefitted the working and middle classes by cutting taxes and increasing investment opportunities.

D. Despite Reagan's tax cuts, the government was able to fund all social programs, so lower income Americans who used them were unaffected by changes in revenue.

Answer:

B. **Correct.** Low taxes on the wealthy were thought to encourage investment in the economy; as a result, wealth would "trickle down" to other Americans. In practice, lower taxes meant less government revenue, and many social programs were cut.

30) **Which best describes the Bush doctrine of preemption?**

A. The US believed that in order to contain terrorism, it had to occupy countries that might harbor terrorists.

B. Fearing that the entire Middle East would succumb to terrorists, the Bush administration established a presence in the centrally located country of Iraq to avoid a "domino effect" of regime collapse.

C. The Bush administration justified international intervention and foreign invasion without previous provocation in order to preempt possible terrorist attacks.

D. The US held prisoners captured during the War on Terror at Guantanamo Bay, where they were not treated as prisoners of war under the Geneva Conventions.

Answer:

C. **Correct.** Preemption was used to justify the 2003 invasion of Iraq, on the assumption that Iraq had weapons of mass destruction it intended to use or to provide for terrorist attacks against the United States.

3

Texas History

According to the US Census as of July 2015, Texas is the second-largest state in the United States with a population of over 27.4 million; it is also the second-fastest growing state in the country. Major Texas cities like Houston, Austin, San Antonio, and Dallas-Fort Worth are among the top ten fastest growing cities in the nation. Furthermore, with a land area of 268,596 square miles, Texas is second in geographical size only to Alaska. With a rich and unique history, ruled

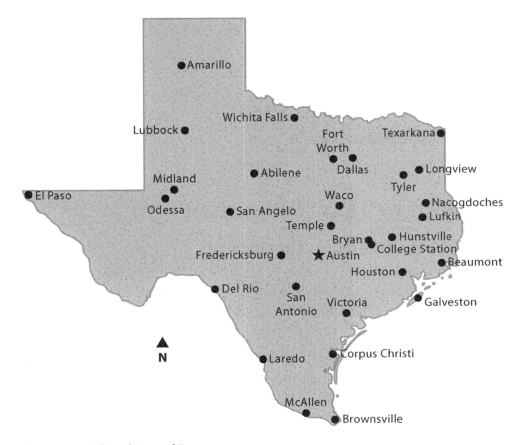

Figure 3.1. Political Map of Texas

by "six flags"—six different countries, including an independent Republic of Texas—and a singular place in the United States today, the state of Texas has a distinctive story to tell. Indeed, understanding the history of Texas is key to understanding the history of the United States—and even North America—as a whole.

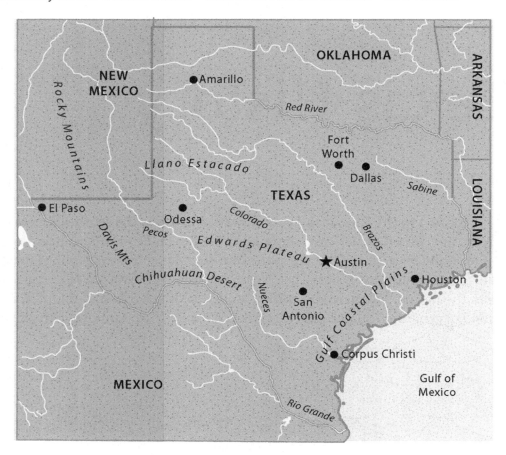

Figure 3.2. Physical Map of Texas

PRECOLONIAL TO TEXAS REVOLUTION

TEXANS BEFORE EUROPEAN CONTACT

Before the arrival of European explorers and colonists, Texas was populated by a number of Native American tribes. The migratory **Karankawa** lived along the Gulf Coast; fishers and hunter/gatherers, they moved via canoe and were among the first to encounter Europeans.

Farther inland, the **Caddo** dominated East Texas, living in settled communities and practicing agriculture throughout the region and in the area around the Red River. Organized in the **Hasinai** alliance, the Caddo engaged in brisk trade, and Europeans took part in this economy. Many Caddo died from diseases introduced by European settlers.

Farther west, tribes like the **Comanche**, **Apache**, and **Kiowa** dominated the Great Plains and moved into northern and western Texas. These migratory tribes adopted horses after the introduction of these animals by Europeans. Violent encounters between these tribes and European, Mexican, Texan, and American settlers were common until the late nineteenth century.

SPAIN IN TEXAS

Spain's search for gold in the Americas spurred its exploration throughout the region north to Texas. In 1519 the Spanish explorer who discovered Texas, **Alonso Àlvarez de Piñeda**, recommended colonization (though he never actually set foot on the land, only viewing it from his ship as he explored the Gulf Coast). An expedition to Florida led by **Pánfilo Naváez** became stranded on the Texas coast after attempting to return to Mexico; seven years later, the survivors, led by **Cabeza de Vaca**, were rescued. Returning to Mexico, they passed on rumors of gold farther inland in Texas, inspiring exploratory expeditions by **Francisco Vasquez de Coronado** and **Hernando de Soto** in 1540, and **Juan de Oñate** in 1598. None were successful in the search for gold, but they did confirm that the land was suitable for raising cattle.

Ultimately, Texas was less valuable than Mexico and other territories because it proved devoid of gold and silver; however Spain was wary of French incursions southwestward. Consequently, the Spanish established missions and *presidios* to create a buffer zone in Texas to repel French interests in North America. The influential and committed priest **Fray Damian Massanet** founded **Mission San Francisco de las Tejas** near San Antonio in 1690, the first mission in Texas, with **Don Alonzo de León**, governor of the region (at the time called Coahuila and New Philippines).

Missions were important and influential due to the zeal of missionaries, despite their failure to convert Native Americans. **Father Francisco Hidalgo** reached out to the French in spite of the political climate, and Lamothe Cadillac, governor of Louisiana, sent Louis Juchereau de St. Denis to trade in Texas. France and Spain jointly founded six other missions. **Father Antonio Jesus de Margil** controlled the missions of East Texas; however, by the end of the decade, missionaries were becoming disheartened with the difficulty of the work and the reticence of the Native Americans to convert. The 1721 Spanish expedition led by **Marque de Aguayo** reinvigorated Spanish presence in the area, which would remain a buffer zone throughout the eighteenth century.

Following the French and Indian War and the decline of French power in North America, after 1754 the **Marquis de Rubi** issued the **New Regulation of the *Presidios*** moving them to San Antonio. San Antonio thus became the frontier and the presence of *presidios* to the north was reduced. This reorganization would improve consolidation of efforts against the Apache and Comanche, who attacked Spanish outposts from the north and west. However, Spanish control over its territories north of Mexico was tenuous.

To strengthen control over Texas, **Governor Francisco Bouligny** of Upper Louisiana and **Governor Bernardo de Galvez** of Lower Louisiana secretly agreed to permit white Anglo settlers in Texas as long as they converted to Catholicism and became Spanish subjects. The **Spanish Conspiracy** was in violation of policy that only encouraged Spanish immigration to New Spain, but it began to strengthen Texas economically. Whites from the United States began immigrating west in search of opportunities in the region. **Moses Austin** left Connecticut with other settlers for the colony of **New Madrid**, now in Missouri; he prospered mining lead for ammunition in Mine à Breton.

The **Adams-Onís Treaty** of 1819, which delineated the border between the United States and Spain, left New Madrid in US territory. Moses Austin asked the governor in San Antonio for permission to immigrate to Texas and introduce settlers, duplicating the New Madrid model; Spain eventually granted him land and permitted settlement in Texas. However he died in 1821 and his son Stephen Austin would carry out this project.

Meanwhile, other Anglo (white) settlers had been flowing into Texas without explicit permission from Spain. Also known as **filibuster settlers**, they immigrated for personal gain but at the same time furthered a US national policy: westward expansion, or the ideal of Manifest Destiny, regardless of borders.

Mexican Texas

Following Mexican independence from Spain, Mexico established the *empresario* system, in which *empresarios*, or land brokers, were granted cheap land and given six years to bring families to settle it as long as they enforced Mexican law. Anglos were permitted to colonize the land in order to better secure it for Mexico under the **Colonization Law of 1825**.

His family's previous agreements with Spain voided following the revolution, **Stephen F. Austin**, Moses Austin's son and an able diplomat, negotiated the first *empresario* arrangement with the new Mexican government and attracted 300 Anglo families to Texas. Settlers could receive, for a low rate, either 4,000 acres of land for ranching or approximately 177 acres for farming—consequently, many became ranchers. In return, they had to demonstrate evidence of "good reputations" (for example, prove they had no criminal background), convert to Catholicism, and become Mexican citizens. However they would not have to pay taxes for seven years.

Mexico wanted foreign settlers to purchase Texas land at only a thirty-dollar down payment with ten years tax-free to encourage settlement. Yet Anglo settlers did not always consider themselves Mexican and also wanted to bring enslaved persons of African origin, a dilemma because Mexico prohibited slavery. As a result, Mexico began encouraging Mexican settlement in Texas to counter this movement.

Still, by the late 1820s, Anglo settlers outnumbered Mexican settlers and others of Spanish and Spanish-speaking origin (called **Tejanos** and **Tejanas**). Anglo-Tejano relations were active: arguably the strongest example was between Stephen F. Austin and **Martin DeLeon**, the first Mexican *empresario*, from Nuevo Santander. DeLeon and his settlers colonized the land near what is today Victoria, Texas. Austin and DeLeon established active relations, including a postal service, between their colonies.

Tensions were developing between the Mexican government and Anglo-dominated Texas. In 1825, US **President John Quincy Adams** proposed the US purchase of Texas; Mexico rebuffed the offer, increasingly suspicious of Anglo Texan and United States intent in the region. In 1826, following disputes over land rights, the *empresario* Haden Edwards formed an alliance with the Cherokee and led the **Fredonia Rebellion** in northeast Texas, declaring independence from Mexico in protest of revocation of land grants. While unsuccessful, these actions contributed to consolidation of political power over the region.

Following growing tensions and violence in northeast Texas, Mexico passed the **Law of April 6, 1830** placing severe restrictions on Texas. It closed immigration from the United States, severing commercial and family ties with the country. Instead, it further encouraged Mexican and European settlement in Texas in order to counter Anglo settlement; it also provided for customs collections in Texas, augmented military presence in the region, and further restricted slavery.

Some Tejanos were also against the Law of 1830; it threatened their economic interests by interfering with business ties to the United States. They also wanted to separate Texas from the rest of its province (Coahuila) and desired better protection from Native American raids. Furthermore, like many other Mexican citizens, they were resentful of the centralized military dictatorships that had replaced the brief Mexican republic.

The law also settled convicts in Texas; since *empresarios* and colonists had originally needed to demonstrate evidence of good reputations, this caused resentment; so did the fact that colonists now needed to pay taxes (although the seven-year exemption was to end anyway). Finally, instability in the Mexican government alarmed Mexicans, Tejanos, and Anglo Texans alike; Anglo Texans, many of whom maintained strong ties to the United States, were concerned about violent changes of government in Mexico City in contrast with ongoing democratic elections in the United States.

With the introduction of a strong military presence in Texas, violent clashes began throughout the region reflecting tensions between the centralist, military government and federalists. In 1832, the federalist governor of Texas and Coahuila, **Jose Maria Latona** reopened the region to Anglo settlement in violation of the Law of 1830; in response, **Captain Juan (John) Davis Bradburn** arrested his representatives near the border with Louisiana and closed Texas ports. Bradburn and his 150 soldiers had been sent by the Mexican government to occupy Anhuac, near Galveston; although he reopened the ports, he later arrested the Anglo attorney **Willian Barret Travis** and his partner Patrick Jack.

Texans demanded Bradburn release Travis and Jack during the first disturbance of 1832 in the **Turtle Bayou Resolution**, in which they also protested the Law of 1830 and reaffirmed their allegiance to the original **Constitution of 1824**. In response, Colonel Jose de las Piedras left Nacogdoches, where he had been stationed with a force of 350, and relieved Bradburn of command, releasing Travis and Jack. However, Austin had already approached Velasco to take a cannon to use at Anhuac, clashing with Colonel Domingo de Ugartechea, stationed there with a force of 150; this clash marked the second disturbance of 1832 and the first real violence of the Texas Revolution.

Upon returning to Nacogdoches, de las Piedras ordered Texans to turn in their firearms; instead, they attacked him and on August 2, 1832, he surrendered and was taken to San Antonio.

Despite the violence of the **Disturbances of 1832**, Austin presented them as efforts in support of the 1824 constitution to protest government centralization and the Law of 1830. On October 1, 1832 Anglo Texans and some Tejanos held the **Convention of 1832**. Electing Austin as head of the governing council of San Felipe, where they met, they drafted a resolution calling for the establishment of Texas as a separate state of Mexico, for self-rule, and for the repeal of the Law of 1830.

Though the resolution was rejected, Texans tried again at the **Convention of 1833**; in April of that year, fifty-six representatives drafted a resolution asking the Mexican government to end restrictions on slavery in Texas, allow increased Anglo immigration from the United States, provide Texans more protection from the Apaches and Comanche, improve mail service, and separate Texas from Coahuila.

Meanwhile, the Mexican military leader **Antonio López de Santa Anna**, upon becoming president of Mexico, nullified the 1824 constitution (and its similarities to the US constitution) in favor of a more restrictive one that centralized federal power. Santa Anna dissolved the Mexican Congress and state legislatures; he also violently put down rebellions in several Mexican states. Finally, Santa Anna dismissed self-rule in Texas.

Stephen F. Austin traveled to Mexico City to present Texas' proposals to the government directly, and was imprisoned. Even after Mexico repealed the Law of 1830, Texas was still not granted its own statehood.

At the same time, filibuster settlers continued moving from the United States to Texas and tensions continued to rise. General Martin Perfecto de Cos was appointed military commander of the northern Mexican provinces, including Texas and Coahuila. He sent troops to collect customs at Anhuac, spurring more violence when William Travis led volunteers against Mexican military there. In response, de Cos increased military presence in Texas.

By Austin's release and return to Texas in 1835, tensions were building toward rebellion.

1) **How did the Law of 1830 reflect tensions between Texas and the Mexican government?**

   A.   The law was intended to protect Tejanos from Anglos.

   B.   Mexico would no longer tolerate the practice of slavery.

   C.   External threats to Mexican control of Texas inspired the Law of 1830; this established a new *empresario* system whereby Mexico could settle Mexicans and Europeans in the region, rather than attracting whites from the United States.

   D.   Anglo dominance in Texas, strong ties with the United States, weak identification with Mexico, and the US policy of westward expansion threatened Mexican control over Texas.

   Answer:

   D.   Correct. From the perspective of the Mexican government, Mexico was losing control of Texas to Anglo interests allied with the United States, and possibly losing Texas to that country. The Law of 1830 was intended to consolidate Mexican control over the region.

REVOLUTION TO STATEHOOD

THE TEXAS REVOLUTION

The refusal of Colonel John H. Moore and his company to return a cannon to the Mexican military at the **Battle of Gonzales** on October 2, 1835 (wheeling it out with the flag *Come and Take It*) is generally considered the beginning of the Texas Revolution. More volunteers assembled and continued to San Antonio, intending to take the city and de Cos.

The volunteers besieged the city; **Ben Milam** led the assault that began the **Battle of San Antonio** (December 5 – 10, 1835) after which de Cos surrendered.

During the siege, delegates met to determine the way forward. They chose **Sam Houston**, the former governor of Tennessee, to lead an army; however other armed groups of volunteers had already sprung up under **James Bowie** in San Antonio, **James Fannin** in Goliad, and elsewhere. As a result, Houston had difficulty organizing and imposing authority beyond the northeast.

By February 1836, Santa Anna himself entered Texas with 6,000 troops in an attempt to subdue the uprising. On February 23, San Antonio was besieged again. Meanwhile, during the chaos fifty-nine delegates, among them two Tejanos, signed the **Texas Declaration of Independence** on March 1, 1836 at Washington-on-the-Brazos. Adopting it the next day, they also wrote the first **Texas Constitution**. The delegates confirmed Sam Houston's command of the army and appointed **David Burnet** as interim president of the Republic of Texas.

A few days later, on March 6 Santa Anna attacked the Alamo. **David Crockett**, a former Tennessee congressman and volunteer colonel and William B. Travis led the defense against Santa Anna (James Bowie was either dead or dying at the time within the Alamo), but ultimately Mexico prevailed in the **Battle of the Alamo**; those not killed in the attack were executed, aside from a few whom Santa Anna freed to warn other Texans.

Figure 3.3. Detail of a Mural Depicting the *Come and Take It* **Flag at Gonzales, Texas**

Upon hearing the news in Gonzales and facing the Mexican advance, Sam Houston evacuated the city in the **Runaway Scrape**. Meanwhile, James Fannin remained at Goliad despite orders to join Houston; defeated by Santa Anna, Fannin's army was executed, too.

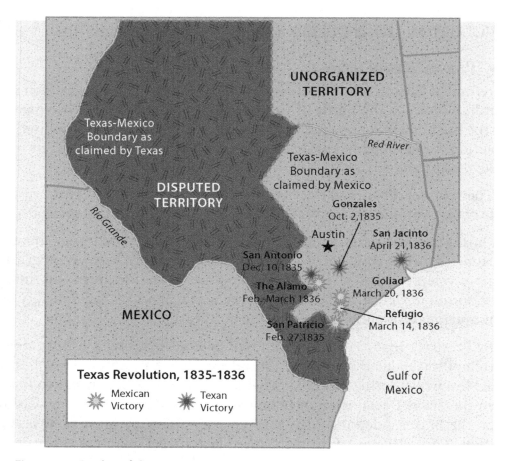

Figure 3.4. Battles of the Texas Revolution

Santa Anna pursued Houston, who moved north. On April 20, Houston's and Santa Anna's forces briefly met on the battlefield at the San Jacinto River and White Oak Bayou.

The next day, during the **Battle of San Jacinto**, Houston surprised the Mexicans by attacking in the afternoon rather than the morning. Lasting only eighteen minutes, the battle was won by the Texans. Houston's army captured Santa Anna and while nine Texans died, an estimated 630 Mexicans were killed.

A few weeks later, on May 14, Santa Anna agreed to the **Treaty of Velasco**, which granted Texas independence. Texas thus became an independent republic.

THE REPUBLIC OF TEXAS

Sam Houston was elected President of the Republic of Texas in September, 1836; **Mirabeau Lamar** became vice president; and Stephen Austin became secretary of state. Land near the village of Waterloo (more centrally located than Houston) was chosen as the location for the new capital, which was named Austin in honor of the secretary of state, who had died shortly after taking office.

Houston had been elected in a landslide, despite running against Austin; many voters were recent immigrants from the United States who were familiar with him from his military and political service there, and were not familiar with Austin's deep history in Texas.

The Republic faced major challenges. Texas was bankrupt and in enormous debt—over one million dollars—with only five hundred dollars in the treasury at one point. Houston established rangers and militia in place of a costly army and enforced customs collections at Galveston. He also sold the Texan naval fleet. His successor, Mirabeau Lamar, printed three million dollars in currency, causing its value to plummet and making his planned investments in infrastructure impossible.

To raise income, Texas continued to exploit its greatest resource: land. The Houston administration gave land away and even issued **land scrip**, a currency redeemable in land, in order to attract settlers. The goal was to raise national income by taxing landowners. Lamar reintroduced the *empresario* system, and attracted more immigrants from the north, including recent arrivals to the United States from Europe. Texans of German and Czech heritage live in east-central Texas to this day, around New Braunfels and LaGrange.

As new settlers of European descent arrived in Texas, relationships between people of different ethnicities changed. In the new republic, only male Anglos and Tejanos were considered citizens; black people (whether enslaved or free), native North Americans, and

CONSIDER THIS

Samuel McCulloch Jr. had fought in the Texas Revolution and was wounded at Goliad; however, he was deprived of Texas citizenship because he was a free black man.

women of any ethnicity were not. According to the Constitution, free black men and women could not even live in the country.

Rapidly rising numbers of white immigrants saw Tejanos as a threat or as Mexican agents. Meanwhile, Texas' relationship with Mexico remained unstable. In 1842 Mexico raided Texas and occupied San Antonio twice. In response, Texas raided the northern Mexican towns of Laredo and Guerrero. Meanwhile, Texas maintained its small naval force of schooners in the Gulf of Mexico in order to protect trade routes with New Orleans; it also provided support to Yucatan when it rebelled against the Mexican government. As Texas' relationship with Mexico deteriorated, new white settlers believed Tejanos—even those who had supported the revolution—to be a threat. Many Tejanos were forced to leave or face a reduced quality of life, living as second-class citizens in an environment of prejudice.

CONSIDER THIS

Juan Erasmo Seguin was unfairly accused of leading the Mexican attack on the city because of his ethnicity; Seguin had been a captain in the Texas army, a senator in the Texas congress, and mayor of San Antonio.

Tense relations also persisted between Texas and Native American tribes. Although Houston had maintained a stable relationship with the Cherokee in the east, Lamar forcibly removed the Cherokee from their land; he also sent military into Comanche land to protect Anglo settlements.

Texas' foreign relations and borders were also complex. In an attempt to extend its sovereignty to the Rio Grande in New Mexico, Texas troops were halted by the US Army in 1843. However, Texas had a strong relationship with the United States; Sam Houston had fought with the current President Andrew Jackson in the War of 1812; under Jackson, the United States had recognized the Republic of Texas in 1837. Jackson, a proponent of Manifest Destiny, was strongly in favor of Texas joining the Union. However, abolitionists were not, given that slavery was an entrenched institution in Texas.

Houston supported joining the United States; Lamar did not, envisioning Texas as a North American power rivalling the US and Mexico alike. While Texas did establish relations with Great Britain, the Netherlands, and France, Houston and others recognized that the United States, its policy of westward expansion, and its ideal of Manifest Destiny would be threatened by any strong relationships between Texas and European powers, particularly Great Britain.

DID YOU KNOW?

Sam Houston had lived with the Cherokee in his youth and even been married to a Cherokee woman; he supported diplomacy in relations with Native Americans, not violence or removal.

Fearful of a Texan alliance with Great Britain, the Tyler administration was open to annexation, and President Houston encouraged President John Tyler in this venture. Tyler first proposed annexation in the form of a treaty; however, treaties must be ratified by the US Senate, which rejected it. Before leaving office, Tyler again proposed annexation to Congress as a joint resolution; this time, the resolution passed. On the Texan side, Congress approved annexation on July 4, 1845; the people confirmed their approval in October. On February 19, 1846, Texas joined the United States as the twenty-eighth state.

ANNEXATION AND THE US–MEXICAN WAR

Texas became a state during the administration of President James Polk. For the United States, annexation was part of its policy of westward expansion. Texas' population grew exponentially, with settlers coming mainly from the South—including enslaved people.

Viewing annexation as a provocation, Mexico recalled its ambassador from the United States. Mexico sent troops to the Rio Grande under the command of General Mario Arista; President Polk sent troops under the command of General Zachary Taylor to the Nueces River 200 miles north. Finally, clashes on April 24, 1846 triggered the **Mexican-American War**. After two years of conflict, the United States and Mexico negotiated the **Treaty of Guadalupe Hidalgo**, in which the United States gained territory including New Mexico, Arizona, Colorado, Utah, Nevada, and California in exchange for fifteen million dollars. Mexico would also abandon any claims to Texas. That same year, Zachary Taylor became president.

Under the Treaty of Velasco, the Rio Grande had formed the boundary between Texas and Mexico; with US gains following the war with Mexico, Texas saw fit to claim land as far west as parts of New Mexico and Colorado as part of the state, in keeping with that treaty. However New Mexicans, with a more entrenched regional history and cultural identity, resisted. At the same time, westward expansion continued to drive debate over slavery in the United States. The American people and government were fiercely divided over whether or not to permit slavery in the enormous new territory obtained following the war.

In the **Compromise of 1850**, Congress agreed to admit California as a free state, with slavery to be decided by popular sovereignty in the Utah and New Mexico Territories. It also strengthened the Fugitive Slave Act but abolished the slave trade in

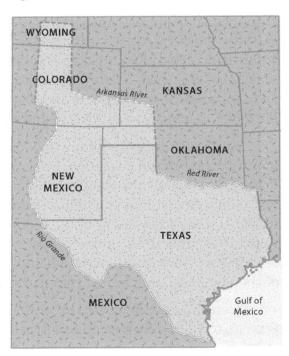

Figure 3.5. Texas' Borders Following the Compromise of 1850

Washington, D.C. Finally, it established the borders of Texas as they stand today, in exchange for ten million dollars to the state of Texas. Given that the US government had not taken on Texas' public debt at annexation, the state benefitted from the arrangement.

THE STATE OF TEXAS

James Pickney Henderson had been elected the first governor of Texas following annexation, and the state was organized in accordance with a constitution written during the last year of the Republic under the guidance of **Thomas Jefferson Rusk**, with many similarities to the US Constitution. It maintained protections for **slavery** and also retained the **Homestead Law**, which prohibited the seizure of indebted owners' property and protected women's property rights. Rusk and Sam Houston were elected to represent Texas in the US Senate. Henderson appointed **John Hemphill** as the first chief justice of the Texas Supreme Court. Meanwhile, Texas' population continued to grow, primarily via the migration of white southerners and their slaves.

HELPFUL HINT

While most new Texans were southerners, many were new immigrants from Europe, including Czechs, Poles, French, Swiss, and numerous Germans; their cultural heritage persists to this day in central Texas, where some locals spoke German as a first language into the 1970s.

Galveston became the largest city in Texas (with approximately 6,000 inhabitants) and an important American port—some claimed it would rival New Orleans and New York City. As the largest port in Texas, Galveston was the gateway for Texas goods, including cotton, sugar and molasses, cattle, and cattle products, which were in demand elsewhere in North America and in Europe. Galveston received manufactured goods, luxury imports (like clothing), furniture, tools and early industrial implements, and enslaved African and African American people.

Texas used the funding from the Compromise of 1850 to settle debts and invest in infrastructure and education. Under the administration of **Governor Elisha M. Pease** (1853 – 1859), the state invested in roads, improvement in river navigability and management, and education. Texas also sought ways to lower taxes for its residents, a tradition that continues. Pease requested a US military presence in the state to protect settlers on the frontier from attacks by the Kiowa, Comanche, and other Native Americans; migration into Texas, mainly from the South, had tripled during the 1850s, and the institution of slavery became more entrenched as a result.

Meanwhile, the entire nation continued to become more divided over slavery. In Washington, Senator Houston voted against the controversial **Kansas-Nebraska Act** of 1854, which opened that territory up to settlement with the legality of slavery to be decided by popular sovereignty, essentially nullifying the Missouri Compromise of 1820 which had forbidden slavery north of the thirty-sixth parallel. At the time,

US senators were chosen by state legislatures (direct election of senators would not take effect until the ratification of the Seventeenth Amendment in 1913). Disapproving of Houston's vote, the Texas State Legislature indicated it would not return him to office, so he returned to Texas to run for governor.

Despite his anti-slavery position, which clashed with supporters of states' rights who believed in the rights of states to determine the legality of slavery, Houston was elected as governor of Texas in 1859.

SAMPLE QUESTION

2) **Following the Texas Revolution, whom of the following were considered citizens of the Republic of Texas?**

A. African American, Tejano, and white men

B. Tejano and white men only

C. Tejano and white men and women

D. white men and women only

Answer:

B. **Correct.** Only Tejano and white men were entitled to citizenship of the Republic of Texas. African American men and women, Tejano women, white women, and Native American men and women were all disqualified from citizenship due to their race and/or gender.

CIVIL WAR AND RECONSTRUCTION

DIVISION AND SECESSION

Most white Texans, whether or not they themselves enslaved other people, supported that practice: many believed in notions of white supremacy, aspired to slave ownership, or refused federal oversight of state laws at all costs. Therefore in the elections of 1860, opposition to Abraham Lincoln and the Republicans was widespread among those able to vote—white males. Lincoln was not even listed on the ballot in Texas and an alternative, vehemently pro-slavery candidate, Vice President John Cabell Breckinridge, beat Lincoln's opponent Stephen Douglas in a landslide in the state.

Following Lincoln's victory in the presidential election of 1860, South Carolina quickly seceded, followed by Georgia, Alabama, Mississippi, Louisiana, and Florida. Texas followed shortly thereafter. (After Texas joined, the remainder of the Confederate states—Arkansas, Virginia, North Carolina, and Tennessee—followed once war broke out.)

Governor Houston opposed secession, but secessionist leaders like John M. Ford called for special elections for delegates to a convention to consider it; elections were held on January 8, 1861. Most delegates were slave owners and many were already state representatives; the convention was scheduled for January 28.

Despite calling an extraordinary meeting of the legislature on January 21 in order to prevent a convention, Houston was essentially without recourse; the legislature failed to act, and the **Secession Convention**, led by **Oran M. Roberts**, later voted overwhelmingly for an **Ordinance of Secession** (with a vote of 166 to eight) on February 1. Texans ratified the ordinance in a special vote on February 23; it passed by 44,317 to 13,020, with only a few counties near the Red River and German-dominated Central Texas voting against. The Secession Convention also wrote a new constitution, specifically stipulating the legality of slavery. A few weeks later, Texas troops forced the Union General David E. Twiggs to surrender at the Alamo; military supplies were taken for Texas.

Texas had not yet joined the Confederacy, and at the time was temporarily once again an independent country. On March 2, Texas Independence Day, secessionists met in Austin to officially declare secession from the United States and allegiance to the Confederate States of America. Governor Sam Houston refused to pledge allegiance to the Confederacy and was replaced by **Lieutenant Governor Edward Clark**, despite his decades of service. Finally, Texas sent observers to attend the meeting of Confederate delegates in Montgomery, Alabama, determining the organization of the Confederacy.

TEXAS AT WAR

While no major fighting took place in Texas, many Texans participated in the Confederate army: 60,000 to 70,000 served, and most were volunteers. Battle did, however, occur in New Mexico. Jefferson Davis permitted Brigadier General Henry Hopkins Sibley to invade the Union Southwest in search of gold in Colorado and in an effort to extend Confederate territory to the Pacific. Having raised a force composed primarily of Texans, Sibley defeated the Union at Valverde and held Santa Fe; however the Texans were forced to retreat from New Mexico after the Union destroyed Sibley's supplies at Glorieta Pass. Consequently, the Confederacy abandoned its designs on the Southwest.

The **Anaconda Plan**, the Union plan to blockade and isolate the Confederacy, and its naval blockade did affect Texas. In October 1862, during the **Battle of Galveston**, the Union army occupied the city, at that time the largest city in mostly rural Texas. However the Confederates recaptured Galveston on January 1, 1863; the Union relinquished control and maintained the blockade successfully from New Orleans. The Confederacy continued to export cotton surreptitiously through Mexico and Cuba. But ongoing shortages of medicine, mechanical and farming tools, coffee, clothing, shoes, and other necessities strained the people of Texas and the state's economy.

The Confederacy surrendered at Appomattox on April 9, 1865. Even though the South had surrendered, the final battle of the Civil War took place a month later near Brownsville—the **Battle of Palmito Ranch**, in which Confederate troops fought arriving Union troops.

On June 19, slavery ended in Texas when US General Gordon Granger enforced the Emancipation Proclamation. Despite Lincoln's announcement in 1863, news of emancipation had not carried to blacks in Texas—slave owners who knew of the decree kept silent. **Juneteenth** is celebrated today in honor of the end of slavery in the state.

RECONSTRUCTION

After the war, Texas suffered economically like much of the South. Given the wartime disruption of production and markets, the devaluation of investments, real estate, stocks, bonds, and currency following the collapse of the Confederacy, and economic uncertainty as Reconstruction loomed, the state faced a depression.

At the same time, societal change gripped the state. The end of slavery was a time of uncertainty. President Lincoln's assassination, the limitations of his Ten Percent Plan, and division in Congress between Radical Republicans seeking retribution from the South, and more moderate Republicans and Democrats, muddled the way forward for Reconstruction.

Like most former Confederate states, Texas refused to ratify the **Fourteenth Amendment**, which provided equal protection under the law to American males regardless of race, recognizing African Americans as US citizens. Consequently, Congress implemented the **Reconstruction Acts** of 1867, which placed the South, including Texas, under military control. Texas was part of **Military District Number Five**, as were Arkansas and Louisiana. At the same time, migration continued into Texas.

While much of the pro-Confederacy Texas establishment bristled under Reconstruction, life began to improve for others. **General Charles Griffin**, who controlled Texas for the Union, ordered elections for delegates to a state constitutional convention. He also appointed former governor Elisha M. Pease to that office again, until a state government could be reestablished.

> **DID YOU KNOW?**
>
> Republicans from the North were scornfully called "carpetbaggers" by supporters of the Confederacy; Southerners who worked with them were derisively referred to as "scalawags."

Because many white supporters of the Confederacy refused to participate, Radical Republicans were largely elected and gathered to write a new state constitution in 1868 (as were ten African Americans); they ratified the Fourteenth Amendment (as well as the **Thirteenth Amendment**, which abolished slavery). Texas was readmitted into the Union on March 30, 1870.

Meanwhile, the federally supported **Freedmen's Bureau** was established to assist newly freed African American men and women. Despite the end of slavery, black men and women faced discrimination and violence, especially from white supremacist groups that formed throughout the South like the **Ku Klux Klan**. Furthermore, many had little or no possessions, skills, or education. The Freedmen's Bureau offered supplies, schooling, and support in finding homes and paid jobs.

Social and agricultural systems were slow to change. Many of those African Americans who remained in Texas became **sharecroppers**, frequently on the land they had previously worked and for the same landowners. The landowner lent land and equipment; the sharecropper provided labor and kept about one-quarter of the harvest—part of which had to be repaid in order to cover the debt for renting the equipment and land. Given the inadequacy of their final yield for consumption and profit, sharecroppers became bound to the system in a cycle of debt and dependency.

Some sharecroppers and others managed to become tenant farmers under the **share tenant system**, in which tenants provided their own labor and tools while working the owner's land, and thus were able to keep more of the harvest. However, tenants often required still more capital to invest in better implements or to survive a poor harvest. The **crop-lien system** allowed them to borrow from outside creditors, but forced them to repay the creditor first at harvest, regardless of the yield. This could put them in more debt and still tied them to the land.

Republican **Governor Edmund Davis**, who had been elected in 1869, was opposed by those Texans who had supported the Confederacy. Known as **Redeemers**, they wanted to "redeem" Texas from outside control. In 1873 Davis was voted out of office, replaced by the Democrat **Richard Coke**. Coke reinstated former Texan leaders like Oran Roberts. The former leader of the Secession Convention, Roberts was appointed by Coke as the chief justice of the Texas Supreme Court.

DID YOU KNOW?

Women's voting rights were not even mentioned in the Constitution of 1876; women would have to continue to fight for the right to vote in Texas as well as in the rest of the United States.

Redeemers had also been outraged by the new, Republican-written constitution, which they believed gave the governor too much power. Coke called for another constitutional convention, this one dominated by Democrats. The resulting **Constitution of 1876**, which replaced the Republican Constitution, decentralized power and limited the power of the state legislature. It remains the state constitution to this day, although over 400 amendments have been added to it. The Democratic Party dominated Texas following Reconstruction until well into the twentieth century.

THE FRONTIER

Unlike most of the former Confederacy, Texas was a frontier state in addition to a southern one, and violent clashes with Plains tribes continued. Disorganization in the west triggered by years of political instability at the state and national levels required the attention of law enforcement; the **Texas Rangers** focused on managing domestic conflict rather than the Native American threat. Union troops stationed in Texas concentrated on carrying out federal policy and Reconstruction away from the Frontier. Kiowa and Comanche became stronger and raiding became more profitable thanks to *comancheros*, who provided them with supplies in exchange for goods stolen from raids on settlements; comancheros then sold these goods on the market farther north or in Mexico. In central Texas, African American contingents (called **buffalo soldiers** by Native Americans) were assigned to protect roads and outposts.

> **DID YOU KNOW?**
>
> Resisting movement to reservations, the Comanche leader Quanah Parker led an alliance of Comanche, Kiowa, and Cheyenne warriors against white buffalo hunters in 1874. Defeated by US forces after a year of conflict known as the Red River War, Quanah Parker became a leader in the reservation system and advocated for the Comanche at the national level.

During the late nineteenth century, the federal government was taking action against Native American tribes in order to capture the Frontier, and Texas was no exception. As it organized the reservation system and continued campaigns against tribes throughout the Great Plains, the federal government came to focus more on Texas following the **Salt Creek Massacre**. Comanche and Kiowa led by **Satanta**, attacked US military near Fort Worth in 1871, triggering an overwhelming response led by **General William T. Sherman**. At the same time, massive **buffalo** hunts continued, destroying Native American ways of life. US legislation like the **Dawes Act** of 1887 continued to subdue Plains tribes. By the end of the nineteenth century, ongoing violence between settlers and Native Americans ultimately resulted in the destruction of tribal societies in Texas as in other states in the country.

Hunting buffalo was especially impactful in Texas because it allowed the development of the **cattle** industry. Both cattle and buffalo flourished on the same land; the fewer buffalo using resources, the more available for cattle.

SAMPLE QUESTION

3) **The Redeemers were able to**

   A. reinstate several prominent, pro-secession Texans to public office after the war.

   B. write a new constitution.

   C. ensure that the Democrats regained power after the Civil War.

   D. all of the above

Answer:

D. Correct. All of the above answer choices are true.

POSTWAR DEVELOPMENT

From 1870 to 1900, Texas politics, economics, and society would change rapidly. Population grew from just over 800,000 Texans in 1870 to over three million Texans in 1900, making Texas the sixth largest state. More people moved to cities. The population of non-whites declined in comparison to whites, as white migrants moved to the state and as non-whites—particularly African Americans—left Texas and the South in search of opportunities elsewhere in the United States as part of the Great Migration. Finally, the number of foreign-born Hispanic Texans—mainly born in Mexico—increased.

Texas' population growth has been possible because of its tremendous wealth. The state is rich in natural resources which helped attract settlement. The economy has continued to grow over decades as natural resources were (and are) further discovered, developed, and exploited.

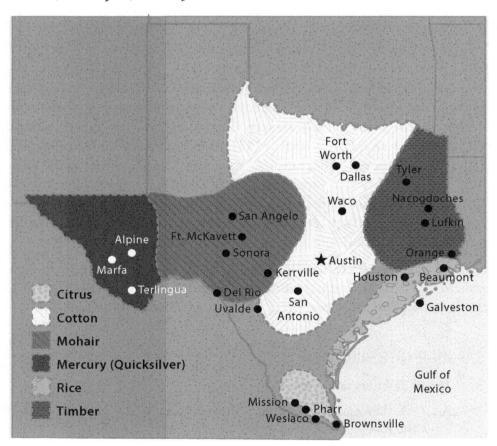

Figure 3.6. Major Texas Products by Region

CATTLE AND RANCHING

Following the Civil War, the Texas economy began to grow—thanks in great part to cattle. A wartime halt to trade had allowed a surplus of Texas cattle to develop; **Joseph G. McCoy** built the first "cow town," Abilene, Kansas, to receive cattle and ship them east to markets via train. This marked the beginning of the cattle trade; cattle were driven north to receiving areas, for railroads had not yet been built farther south or east than Missouri and parts of Kansas. **Cattle drives** became an industry dominated and organized by contractors who led organized teams ensuring the security and progress of the animals. The ideal of the frontier cowboy took root in American folklore, but cattle-driving as an industry was short lived.

Cattle originated in southern Texas, but major ranches, or "spreads," appeared throughout the state, some of which still exist. The **King Ranch**, founded in 1853 by Richard King and Mifflin Kennedy, is one of the largest; still in use today for hunting and tourism, it encompasses more land than the state of Rhode Island. The **Matador Ranch**, based in the Texas Panhandle, historically included parcels of land throughout the Great Plains as far north as the Canadian border, and its remnants exist today as part of a larger corporation.

Ranching continued (and continues) to be a major part of the Texas economy; however, cattle drives only lasted until the end of the nineteenth century. Cattle drives were no longer necessary as meatpacking facilities opened in Texas' growing cities and as railroads extended farther west and into Texas itself. However, the development of railroads would only add to Texas' own economic growth.

RAILROADS

Initially, most railroads centered on Houston and Galveston; the **Houston, East & West Texas Railroad (HE&WT)** connected Houston and Shreveport, Louisiana. Meanwhile, the first major east-west and north-south railroad crossing was built in Dallas. Eventually lines like the Kansas City Southern, Missouri Pacific, Santa Fe Regional, Texas & New Orleans, and Cotton Belt crossed the state. Existing lines like the Kansas City Southern and Union Pacific continue to do so. Crossings and construction sites gave rise to towns like Lufkin.

The construction of transcontinental railroads throughout the United States included development in Texas. Texas' geography made the state key to railroad development, and Grenville Dodge began construction of the **Texas and Pacific Railroad** in 1869 in Marshall, Texas. Jay Gould—a New York City "robber baron"— took over the T&P in Dallas in 1874, completing construction across the state to El Paso. There, the T&P connected with the **Southern Pacific**, which originated in San Diego. The Southern Pacific was able to use track to cross Texas to reach New Orleans. As a result, Texas became integral to continental rail transportation and trade.

TIMBER

Given the size of the state, by 1904 over 10,000 miles of track had been laid; the subsidized industry was growing exponentially like many others. Railroads helped trigger economic development in small and widely dispersed towns: businesses relocated to areas that were easy to access, and population centers that attracted railroad companies grew.

Railroad construction also spurred development of the **timber industry** in East Texas. Rich in pine woods, the 68,000 square mile region north of Beaumont was estimated to contain enough wood to produce 300 million board feet of lumber. Cross ties for track were made out of wood, so demand for timber was linked directly to railroad construction. Furthermore, the HE&WT provided a means for Texas timber to reach the rest of the United States and even the world.

The "lumber baron" John H. Kirby's **Kirby Lumber Company** led the exploitation of most of the old growth forest by 1920. Based in Beaumont, the Kirby Lumber Company functioned by constructing and operating mills and company towns throughout the region, maintaining a grasp on the workforce. Smaller companies emerged as well; later movements experimented with sustainable forestry and management of what forest was left.

AGRICULTURE

Railroads were also key in promoting another important agricultural product. The terrain around Houston and Galveston close to the Gulf Coast was suitable for **rice**, and the Houston Chamber of Commerce, in conjunction with the Southern Pacific railroad, promoted rice growth in the area. Louisiana settlers had already been growing rice in the region, but the Houston Chamber of Commerce invited a Japanese scholar studying in the United States to teach Texas farmers more rice-growing techniques. Japanese immigrants in turn came to the region to take advantage of agricultural opportunities. The region produced 99 percent of the US rice by the twentieth century, and the Southern Pacific profited from transporting the product.

Rice was only one of many profitable agricultural products in Texas. Until the late nineteenth century, **cotton seeds** had been discarded in the cotton harvest. Indeed, the cotton gin had been one of the most important inventions of the Industrial Revolution, for it quickly separated the seeds from the fiber, substantially speeding up the process. However, valuable uses for cotton seeds were discovered, including its high levels of nitrogen. The pulp from crushed cotton seeds supplemented animal feed—especially feed for cattle, one of Texas' most valuable products—and was also a powerful fertilizer. Furthermore, oil for industrial lubrication could be extracted from cotton seeds. Cotton was a cash crop in Central Texas; the sharecropper system (see above) in the region was effectively an extension of slavery, allowing maximum exploitation of labor to harvest cotton seeds.

Farther north and west, **wheat** became an important agricultural product. Migrants to Texas—including recent European immigrants—began settling the area after the Civil War, and by the beginning of the twentieth century over 300,000 family farms were established in the plains regions of the state. Irrigation, crop diversification, and farming methods that allowed for maximum absorption of water enabled farmers to coax crops from the rough terrain. Eventually, better farming technology improved agriculture in the region; the discovery of the Ogallala Aquifer improved irrigation. However, the drought and Dust Bowl phenomenon of the 1930s harmed farmers throughout the Great Plains, and Texans were no exception.

Later in the early twentieth century, **citrus** products would become important in South Texas. While the Rio Grande Valley region seemed unsuitable for agriculture, in 1912 a pharmacist from Iowa, **John Harry Shary** acquired land, irrigated it, and planted citrus trees, successfully growing **grapefruit**. Meanwhile, migrant workers moved in the region with their families, finding work in the fields.

OIL

Texas' most famous product, and arguably its lifeblood, is petroleum. In 1901, Patillo Higgins posited that there was oil under a salt hill called **Spindletop** near Beaumont, despite some ongoing production farther north in **Corsicana** since the late nineteenth century. Hiring the Czech engineer Anthony Lucas to drill, Higgins struck oil on January 10; the **Lucas Gusher** would prove to be the largest oil source in the world at that time.

Beaumont would become home to the nascent Texas oil industry. New companies like the Guffey Oil Company (later to become Gulf Oil, and then **Chevron**) and the Texas Oil Company (**Texaco**) opened offices in Beaumont and refineries in Port Neches and Port Arthur. Oil, which demanded specialized equipment like pipelines and drills, developed a new economy of its own; it also energized existing industries like the timber industry.

Figure 3.7. Lucas Gusher

Drilling continued at Spindletop, and in 1926 even more oil was discovered. Investors explored possibilities throughout Texas, and the oil industry developed as wells popped up in Humble, Sour Lake, Batson, and Goose Creek. Eventually exploration in the **Permian Basin**, located on public land in West Texas, yielded considerable revenue, much of which went to support education (including a substantial endowment for the University of Texas).

EARLY TWENTIETH CENTURY

POPULISTS AND PROGRESSIVES

The Populist attorney general **James Stephen Hogg** took office in 1886. Popular with the public, Hogg targeted insurance companies, assisting in lawsuits against insurers that did not meet their obligations and saving Texans over a million dollars. Hogg especially targeted the powerful railroads, which were under attack nationally. Prosecuting railroads that sought to limit or halt unprofitable service to small towns, he also forced railroad companies to invest more in safety.

DID YOU KNOW?

The Texas Railroad Commission also oversees oil and gas matters because petroleum management was not originally believed to be a major issue, nor oil an important resource. So with no one else willing to handle it, that work was handed off to the Railroad Commission.

In 1890, Hogg was elected governor, in part due to his plan to create a **Texas Railroad Commission**. This would be the first state agency created for the purpose of regulating the activities of a specific industry. Hogg appointed the Texas congressman John Henninger Reagan as chairman of the commission; Reagan had himself introduced legislation creating the Interstate Commerce Commission in Congress.

Governor Hogg enforced progressive legislation reining in corporate interests. Known as the **Hogg Laws**, they included forcing corporations to either use or return state property subsidies within a certain time period, and requiring insurance companies to utilize Texas banks when depositing insurance premium payments in order to allow Texas courts to access the funds.

Edward M. House, a wealthy cotton magnate, was extremely influential in Texas politics and helped ensure Hogg's reelection. House also supported subsequent Texas governors who shared Hogg's populist and progressive inclinations.

Texas Progressives unexpectedly gained ground in 1900 when Galveston was hit by a devastating hurricane. **The Galveston Storm** on September 8 of that year killed an estimated 6,000 people, exposing the city's vulnerability to storm surges and flooding. In responding to the crisis, city officials divided responsibilities in a structured fashion that became the foundation for modern city government and planning; city management became separated from legislation.

In 1914, **James E. Ferguson** ran for governor. His broad efforts throughout rural Texas, despite his roots in banking and lack of political experience, propelled him to office. Ferguson focused on the plight of sharecroppers and proposed a farm tenant rent law (that would later prove unsuccessful), to stabilize the yields sharecroppers paid to landowners. As governor, Ferguson continued to focus on the rural poor: the

Rural High School Law assisted schools to pool and improve educational resources, and the state highway department improved Texas roads in time for the advent of the automobile. The state would be able to standardize construction and continue to improve planning.

Nevertheless, scandals wracked the Ferguson administration, and a dispute between Governor Ferguson and Robert Vinson, president of the University of Texas, eventually resulted in the impeachment of the governor by the Texas House of Representatives. Ferguson was found guilty of several improprieties and was to be forbidden from ever again holding public office in the state; however he resigned a day before the legislature's order in order to claim he would still be able to be politically active in the future. Lieutenant Governor **Willian P. Hobby** took over and was reelected in 1918.

Hobby faced a Texas recovering from the First World War, which meant that many working people had returned from fighting overseas, reenergizing the limited labor movement in Texas. Unlike the populist and progressive bent of Ferguson's administration, Hobby acted against labor, including forcing striking dockworkers in Galveston back to work via the Open Ports Law.

A few years later, in 1924 another Ferguson would take office: Jim Ferguson's wife **Miriam "Ma" Ferguson**. One feature of the post-war South, including Texas, was a resurgence of the Ku Klux Klan, which advocated not only racism, but also nativism and Christian fundamentalism. Ferguson took steps to fight the Klan, including supporting anti-mask legislation, which curtailed its activities since it depended on anonymity and secrecy to practice its criminal and racist violence. Governor Ferguson also pardoned an estimated 2,000 convicts.

When Ma Ferguson was elected, women had only been able to vote for four years. Activists including Rebecca Henry Hayes, Annette Finnegan, Eleanor Brackenridge, and Minnie Fisher Cunningham worked to get women the right to vote in Texas. Women could not vote in state primaries until 1918, and then they voted a woman into public office: Annie Webb Blanton became state superintendent of public instruction.

Texas activists were also influential in the ratification of the Nineteenth Amendment, giving women the right to vote nationally. **Jane Y. McCallum** was president of the Austin Woman Suffrage Association, actively working for women's right to vote. Texas was the first state in the South to ratify the Nineteenth Amendment, on June 26, 1919.

In 1929, the **League of United Latin American Citizens (LULAC)** was founded in Corpus Christi to support Mexican American civil rights. Originally composed of small business owners and skilled workers, LULAC addressed civil rights legislation and still works today.

INTERNATIONAL ISSUES

Texas was key to US foreign policy during the early twentieth century. Sharing a long border and history with Mexico, Texas became enmeshed in political tensions that led to the 1910 Mexican Revolution and its impact on the United States.

Mexican revolutionaries fighting the dictator Porfirio Diaz were based in Texas, and the border region bore the brunt of fighting; furthermore, Mexican refugees fled to Texas. Even following Diaz' overthrow, tensions grew as Mexico became unstable.

During the **Tampico Affair** in 1914, a confusing situation led to the arrest of US soldiers by the Mexican military; in retaliation, the United States occupied Veracruz. Attacks on US interests by **Pancho Villa** resulted in limited US military action; however, President Wilson took a conservative approach. Ultimately, the United States became distracted from the situation upon the interception of the **Zimmerman Note**, an invitation from Germany to Mexico to form an alliance in the First World War against the United States. As a result of the publication of the note, the United States entered the war in Europe and the situation with Mexico on the Texas border cooled.

THE GREAT DEPRESSION AND THE NEW DEAL

Texas, like the rest of the country, suffered from the Great Depression. Despite its diversified economy, the state exhibited severe income inequality. Oil, cattle, and cotton "barons" enjoyed great wealth, but the great majority of the state lived paycheck to paycheck, unable to save or invest. Following the First World War, national demand for consumer goods dropped; factories began laying people off. Furthermore, demand for agricultural goods dropped as wartime demand for food and fibrous substances declined. The collapsing price of cotton devastated that industry; over-farming in the Great Plains, combined with a major drought in the 1930s, resulted in the **dust bowl**, crop failures throughout the region, including northern Texas. Farmers were forced to leave their land.

In 1932, Miriam Ferguson was reelected governor of Texas. At the same time, **Franklin Delano Roosevelt** became president of the United States. His **New Deal** legislation was eagerly adopted in Texas and supported by the Ferguson administration.

During FDR's administration, the United States emerged from the Great Depression and entered the **Second World War**. Texas played an important part in the war as home to several military and training bases, as a producer of military ships and aircraft, and as an essential source of petroleum, petroleum products, and synthetic rubber, all necessary for military activity. Texan war leaders included **Col. Oveta Culp Hobby**, who commanded the Women's Army Corps.

SAMPLE QUESTION

4) **Which of the following is an example of the Progressive tradition and movement in Texas?**

   A. Governor Hobby acting to protect striking Galveston dockworkers

   B. legislation restricting corporate behavior and benefitting the rural poor passed during the Hogg and the Ferguson administrations

   C. increased job opportunities for migrant workers in south Texas in the citrus industry

   D. the successful connection of the T&P and Southern Pacific

Answer:

B. Correct. Hogg and the Fergusons were politicians in the Progressive tradition. Hogg was especially known for taking action against big business, and the Ferguson administrations acted in favor of the rural poor.

MODERN TEXAS

POSTWAR TEXAS

As Texas grew, so did its national presence.

The Democrat **Lyndon B. Johnson** was appointed by FDR to run a New Deal program, the National Youth Administration, in Texas in 1935. Two years later, he successfully ran for Congress and represented Texas in Washington. He lost a senatorial campaign in 1941 and served in the military, returning to public office following election to the Senate in 1948 with the defeat of Coke Stevenson in the primaries and Jack Porter in the general election.

A powerful Democrat in Congress and the Senate, LBJ developed a reputation as a "favorite son" and as a legislator who was able to push through legislation working with interests on both sides of the aisle. His sometimes aggressive and controversial style made him a strong voice for Democrats in the Progressive tradition and a strong voice for Texas on the national stage.

Johnson took a strong role in the Civil Rights Act of 1957, foreshadowing civil rights legislation he would preside over in the 1960s as president. He also oversaw 1950s hearing on the space program in the wake of the Soviet launch of Sputnik. LBJ led the National Aeronautics and Space Act of 1958, and he ensured that **NASA** would be based in Houston. In 1960 he was elected vice president on the ticket with John F. Kennedy, and upon Kennedy's assassination in 1963, became president of the United States.

In the Progressive tradition, Johnson's administration saw the passage of liberal legislation in support of the poor and of civil rights. In 1964, Congress passed the **Civil Rights Act**, which outlawed segregation. While according to the Fifteenth

Amendment and the Nineteenth Amendment, all African Americans—men and women—had the right to vote, many Southern states, including Texas, had voting restrictions in place such as literacy tests and poll taxes, which disproportionately affected African Americans. In 1965, led by President Lyndon B. Johnson, Congress passed the **Voting Rights Act**, which forbade restrictions impeding the ability of African Americans to vote, including literacy tests. Separately, the **Twenty-Fourth Amendment** made poll taxes unconstitutional.

> **DID YOU KNOW?**
>
> In 2011, Texas introduced a law forcing voters to show identification in order to cast a ballot, which disproportionately affect the ability of minorities and the poor to exercise their right to vote.

Promising a **Great Society**, LBJ embraced **liberalism**, believing that government should fight poverty at home and play an interventionist role abroad (in that era, by fighting communism). His administration launched a **War on Poverty**, passing reform legislation to support the poor. The **Medicare Act** provided medical care to elderly Americans; the creation of the **Department of Housing and Urban Development** increased the federal role in housing and urban issues. Johnson's **Head Start** program provided early intervention for disadvantaged children before elementary school (and still does today); the **Elementary and Secondary Education Act** increased funding for primary and secondary education. Additionally, the **Immigration Act of 1965** overturned the provisions of the Emergency Quota Act, ending the racist limitations on immigrants to the US.

At the same time, LBJ's overseas agenda was increasingly unpopular. Adhering to containment and Domino Theory—US policy toward communism in an effort to stop its spread—Johnson drew the United States deeper into conflict in Southeast Asia. The **Vietnam War** was extremely unpopular in the US due to high casualties, the unpopular draft (which forced young American males to fight overseas) and what seemed to many to be the purposelessness of the war. Student activists, organizing in the mold of the Civil Rights Movement, engaged in non-violent (and, at times, violent) protest against the Vietnam War.

Deeply unpopular by the end of the 1960s, Johnson announced he would not run for reelection in 1968. He remains a controversial figure in US history, but one of Texas' most important leaders on the national stage.

Civil Rights

As Texas continued to grow, so did its diverse populations, including Hispanic and Mexican-American Texans. Hispanics faced discrimination in public life. **Hector P. Garcia**, a veteran of World War Two, established the **American GI Forum** to ensure access for non-white veterans to the benefits to which they were entitled. Furthermore, Texas remained segregated under **Jim Crow** laws. Many Hispanic Texans were considered "colored" and oppressed as African American Texans were under Jim Crow. All Texans of color struggled against segregation. Consequently, Texan leaders became important voices in the Civil Rights Movement.

In 1956, **Henry B. Gonzalez** became the first Mexican American elected to the Texas Senate. A community leader, Gonzalez organized the Hispanic community and became known as a crusader against segregation on the San Antonio City Council, supporting legislation to desegregate public parks and other areas. During his time in the state legislature, Gonzalez continued to focus on civil rights and fighting segregation, filibustering state efforts to bypass civil rights legislation and reinstitute segregation in schools. Despite considerable opposition, in 1961 Gonzalez, with the support of President Kennedy and Vice President Johnson, was elected to the House of Representatives—the first Texan Hispanic American in Congress. Gonzalez served until 1997.

Figure 3.8. Henry B. Gonzalez

In Washington, Gonzalez supported landmark civil rights legislation and LBJ's Great Society programs. Notably, he opposed the Bracero program, which had provided jobs to migrant Mexican workers beginning in WWII, due to the poor conditions faced by workers under the program.

Texas was also a battlefield in the fight for black civil rights. In 1950, Herman Sweatt, a black man, sued the University of Texas when he was denied admittance to its law school based on his race. Eventually reaching the US Supreme Court, the case *Sweatt v. Painter* forced the desegregation of UT and became precedent for *Brown v. Board of Education*. Thurgood Marshall argued the case, and Sweatt was backed by the National Association for the Advancement of Colored People (NAACP), led in Texas at the time by **Lulu Belle Madison White**, one of the first female leaders of the organization in the South.

Figure 3.9. Barbara Jordan

In 1965, **Barbara Jordan** was elected to the Texas State Senate—the first African American woman in the legislature. Jordan focused on civil rights and equality in employment, lobbying for a minimum wage and the creation of the Fair Employment Practices Commission. Jordan also advocated for anti-discrimination wording in business contracts.

In 1972, for the first time Texans sent a woman and an African American to the House of Representatives when they elected her as a representative. As a member of the House Judiciary Committee, Representative Jordan played an important role during the hearings debating the impeachment of President Richard Nixon due to the Watergate scandal. She also advocated for broader civil rights provisions on the national level. Jordan was only able to serve three terms due to illness; she later took a position at the University of Texas.

FROM BLUE TO RED

At the end of the 1960s, Conservatives became more powerful in the United States; Texas was no exception. Despite giving the country one of its foremost Democrats—LBJ—Texas began to turn from a blue state to a red one.

Conservative working- and middle-class whites who had traditionally supported the Democratic Party in the South became disillusioned after the Johnson administration's support of the Civil Rights movement. Democratic strongholds in the South and in Texas began to turn red; Democrats switched parties and became Republicans.

Meanwhile, Texas continued to grow. More conservative Republicans migrated to Texas suburbs, bringing more Republicans to the state. Conservative Democrats declined in Texas, as they did elsewhere in the United States, so Republicans were more likely to defeat liberal Democrats in moderate-to-conservative districts, putting more Republicans in office throughout the state. While many Democrats remained in power throughout the end of the twentieth century, the trend toward a Republican Texas was rooted in the beginning of the conservative movement in the 1970s.

Also during the 1970s and 1980s, fluctuations in the oil market led to economic change in Texas. The **1973 oil crisis** was triggered by oil-producing Arab countries, which imposed an **oil embargo** on the West in retaliation for its support of Israel during the Yom Kippur War that year. OPEC states inflated oil prices. Consequently, oil-producing areas like Texas experienced huge economic growth as the price of oil skyrocketed. Later, in 1979 the Iranian Revolution deposed the Shah of Iran, a major US ally in the Middle East. As Iran was an important source of world petroleum, instability from the revolution increased prices further, causing the **energy crisis**. Finally, the beginning of the Iran-Iraq War in 1980—a conflict between two major oil producers—further destabilized the market and raised prices.

Dizzying growth in the oil industry brought revenue to Texas, especially Houston. However, during the 1980s, slowed manufacturing and conservation measures taken in response to the 1970s crises resulted in an **oil glut**, and oil prices began to fall. The petroleum industry suffered. Eventually, the energy sector would diversify and invest in natural gas resources throughout Texas and Louisiana.

Texas remained central on the political stage throughout the 1980s as well. **Senator Lloyd Bentsen**, a Democrat, was the vice presidential nominee in 1988. Bentsen was an influential senator and served on the Joint Economic Committee,

Finance Committee, and Campaign Committee; he eventually became Secretary of the Treasury under President Clinton. Bentsen was succeeded by **Senator Kay Bailey Hutchison**, Texas' first female senator. Hutchison served on the Commerce, Science, and Transportation Committee throughout her tenure from 1993 – 2013; she focused on deregulating Amtrak, improving security after the attacks of September 11, 2001, and nurturing NASA and research in STEM (science, technology, engineering, and math).

In 1990, **George W. Bush**, son of the Republican national leader and contemporaneous president George H.W. Bush, ran for governor against the popular Democratic incumbent **Ann Richards**. He would serve as governor until his controversial election to the national presidency in 2000. Bush's governorship emphasized criminal justice, capital punishment, tax cuts, and faith-based social service models. Bush also instituted educational reforms. Some of his state policies influenced later change at the national level, another example of Texas' influence on the country.

Following Bush's election as president, Lieutenant Governor **Rick Perry** took over; he was elected as governor in 2002 and became the state's longest-serving governor, remaining in office until 2015. State government became solidly Republican under Perry's watch; at the same time, urban and suburban populations increased while rural populations decreased. Hispanic and African American populations grew in the first fifteen years of the twenty-first century; white populations declined. Energy production skyrocketed not only in the oil and gas industry but also in wind power, and Texas became a national leader in job growth. Texas also spent more on education.

Recently, **Governor Greg Abbott**, formerly Perry's lieutenant governor, has stirred controversy by supporting even more restrictive measures on women's health than his predecessor and suggesting that US military presence in Texas threatens state sovereignty.

TEXAS TODAY

Today Texas, with its long border with Mexico, remains a flashpoint in the debates over **immigration reform** in the United States. It is estimated that Texas is home to the second-highest population of undocumented immigrants in the country. Many are from Mexico and Central America, but others come from Asia, South America, and elsewhere in the world. The state and the country continue to struggle to find a long-term solution for the millions of people who reside in the United States without visas.

Questions about how to monitor and manage the Mexican border, the humanity of immigrant detention centers where people await deportation—sometimes for years—and the harms of deportation on families when members have different residency statuses remain unresolved. Advocates favor a path to citizenship. Legislation proposed by both Democrats and Republicans at the national level (and even jointly sponsored legislation) has failed. Whatever the outcome, Texas will remain at the forefront of the debate.

Texas is a global leader in **medical research**, with several world class hospitals and research facilities throughout the state, notably in Houston at the Texas Medical Center. People from around the country and the world travel to the state for cutting edge treatment, especially in cancer, children's care, and to access the newest medical technology and medical trials at hospitals like M.D. Anderson Cancer Center, Texas Children's Hospital, and other leading institutions.

Texas is also a national leader and major international player in **technological manufacturing and export**. The state surpasses California in technological manufacturing and generates hard currency by exporting to Mexico. Texas Instruments, Verizon, and other companies in Dallas and San Antonio provide manufacturing jobs for thousands of Texans. The business-friendly climate of the state has encouraged tech startups in the fast-growing cities of Austin, San Antonio, and Houston, where more tech development is under way.

With five of the fastest-growing cities in the country (Houston, Austin, Dallas, Fort Worth, and San Antonio) Texas continues not only to grow in population size, but to experience rapid **urbanization** and its accompanying problems. Overwhelming traffic on freeways built to accommodate far smaller populations, the immediate environmental impact of an influx of people and automobiles on the environment, and long-term concerns about affordable housing and sustainable development continue to challenge the state.

Rapid **suburbanization** as city dwellers and the middle class aspire to homeownership or larger homes beyond urban areas has a negative environmental impact. Suburban sprawl is a feature of the Texas landscape, placing a heavy burden on roads, reservoirs, drainage systems, and other existing infrastructure. The state must find ways to keep up with growth.

Texas remains one of the most economically and politically influential states of the Union; the history of Texas will no doubt continue to have an impact on the history of the United States as a whole in the twenty-first century.

SAMPLE QUESTION

5) **How has modern Texas influenced the United States?**

A. White Texans overwhelmingly supported Johnson's administration.

B. Many influential Texans like Barbara Jordan and Henry Gonzalez were important figures in the Civil Rights Movement.

C. Today, Texas is the national leader in tech manufacturing.

D. B and C only.

Answer:

D. Correct. Choices B and C are both correct.

4

Social Studies Foundations, Skills, Research, and Instruction

I n designing instruction to meet the needs of students, teachers must understand the purpose of teaching social studies and be able to transfer knowledge effectively. To support student learning, teachers must select strategies and resources that address all social studies concepts and content areas.

HISTORY

Understanding **chronology** is essential to student understanding of history at the elementary level. Teachers must cover classical civilizations, US history from **founding** to the twenty-first century, and twentieth century developments and transformations worldwide. To help students understand these events, teachers should select a variety of sources to supplement textbooks, including historical maps, historical photographs, architecture, and political cartoons, to help students deepen their understanding.

Developing chronological thinking is one of the first steps in teaching history; chronologies help students examine relationships between the past and present, the causes and effects of historical events. Teachers help students identify the temporal structure of a historical narrative (e.g. the beginning, middle, and end) so that they can construct their own historical narratives. Students should practice explaining the origins of an event and how it developed over time.

To help students develop chronological thinking, assignments may include creating and interpreting timelines illustrating the differences among the past, present, and future. Teachers should select well-written historical narratives such as biographies and historical literature to supplement class work. These resources enable students to analyze patterns of historical duration (like the legacy of a notable historical document, such as the US Constitution) and historical succession (such as the evolution of broad systems over time, like trade and communication networks).

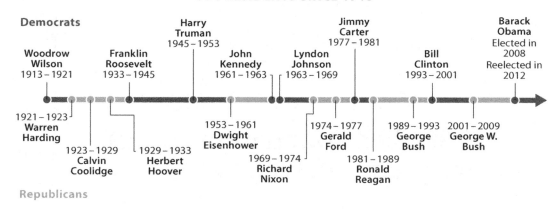

US PRESIDENTS SINCE 1913

Figure 4.1. Presidential Timeline

For students to develop a deeper understanding of history, they cannot simply view it as a series of facts. Students should develop an understanding of **historical analysis**, the interpretation of historical processes, documents and events. The goal is for students to understand not only what happened, but how and why it did.

Historical analysis requires evaluating sources and developing reasonable conclusions based on the evidence gathered. Students need to address multiple perspectives so they can assess whether a source is credible. Teaching students to use primary and secondary sources is integral for them to develop a deeper understanding of the topic being studied.

Students who successfully grasp historical analysis will be able to **analyze** the causes and effects of events. To do so, students can look at both immediate and underlying causes. Immediate causes are what trigger the main event. For example, Japan's surrender in the Second World War was an immediate cause for the war's end. Underlying causes are more likely to be trends that emerged long before the event in question; for instance, sectionalism was an underlying cause of the US Civil War.

Students must learn to compare events from different times and regions and hypothesize how the past influences the present. These comparisons can be as simple as comparing and contrasting Greek inventions with Roman ones, or discussing how Egyptian papyrus influenced how people communicate today.

SAMPLE QUESTIONS

1) **Which of the following is NOT an appropriate example to use in describing a cause or effect of the US Civil War?**

   A.   Inflation grew as more money was printed in both the North and the South.

   B.   European immigrants were attracted to the South because of its booming economy, exacerbating tensions that led to the Civil War.

C.   Cotton exports to England stopped because the Union enforced a naval blockade of the South.

D.   Several states seceded from the Union when Abraham Lincoln became president.

Answer:

B.   Correct. Immigrants from Europe actually preferred the North because there were more job opportunities there.

2)   **A teacher asks students to compare different songs and poems about the War of 1812. In small groups, they must explain how these sources help people understand significant historical events and other people's perspectives on them. This assignment is an example of**

A.   questioning.

B.   chronology.

C.   interpreting timelines.

D.   historical analysis.

Answer:

D.   Correct. This assignment requires students to understand the events of the War of 1812, analyzing primary resources, and then to develop their own conclusions.

Social Studies Skills and Processes

Teaching social studies is not complete without giving students an understanding of the skills and processes they need to be informed and engaged with people in the world around them. Students must be aware that their world is continuously changing; the skills they learn in social studies enable them to cope with social change and thrive in society. Teachers must deliver social studies content in a way that students can understand; furthermore, teachers must help students develop their written and oral abilities to communicate their interpretations of current and historical events. Instructional strategies should address economic reasoning, chronological and spatial thinking, and historical interpretation by having students evaluate primary and secondary sources.

To do so, teachers should help students understand **information analysis**. Students consider an issue at hand and gather information to help them approach the issue. Lessons should address how students can find information, including appropriate materials, **text resources**, and technology to use in the inquiry process. Students should also learn the difference between primary and secondary resources, their advantages and disadvantages, and when it is appropriate to use them. For example, students should understand that **photographs** are considered a primary resource; they depict an original perspective on an event. The overall message should be that students need a variety of sources to best understand the topic being discussed.

Teachers should also help students determine the credibility of sources. For example, the Internet provides a wealth of information, but not everything that a student finds may be relevant or true. Students should understand that determining online credible resources requires knowledge of the author and his or her reputation, whether the domain name is linked to a reputable organization, and whether other references are cited (e.g. peer-reviewed articles and other appropriate authoritative sources).

The next step is learning to organize research to ensure it is relevant. Students should gain exposure to different kinds of social science resources and develop the skills needed to interpret and understand various types of information. For example, if students are studying deforestation, they might need to gather **maps**, **datasets**, or **images** that show how many trees have been cut down over a certain amount of time. Such projects can be used in lessons to illustrate the value of specific resources and how to find them.

From there, students should learn how to organize and **synthesize** information: social science students must process and interact with information rather than just regurgitating it. Here, strong reading comprehension skills are essential; furthermore, students should learn to closely examine data for repeating patterns and trends. Teachers help students to apply new knowledge to gain new insights.

Graphic organizers like **diagrams**, **tables**, and **graphs** help visually impart information, allowing students to identify variables or values affecting relevant data and determine the pros and cons of issues.

Popular types of graphic organizers include Venn diagrams (comparing and contrasting issues), semantic webs (to help students brainstorm ideas), mind maps, KWL charts (where students write down what they know, want to know, and want to learn about a given topic), and concept circles (in which students categorize words related to a certain topic). Graphic organizers also help students develop decision-making skills: students learn to take into account values, different courses of action, and potential consequences. As a result, teachers guide students toward better decision-making in their own lives.

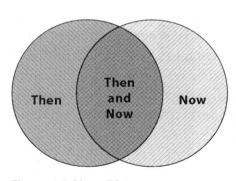

Figure 4.2. Venn Diagram

SAMPLE QUESTIONS

3) **Which of the following would be the most appropriate graphic organizer for a student who is asked to organize a series of significant events?**

A. KWL chart

B. timelines

C. Venn diagram

D. semantic web

Answer:

B. **Correct.** Timelines allow students to sequence events, organizing their thoughts.

4) **Which of the following is NOT a method teachers should encourage students to use when conducting online research?**

A. selecting appropriate keywords

B. looking through a website for relevant information

C. checking the validity of the source by researching its author or publisher

D. choosing the first search result as a valid source

Answer:

D. **Correct.** Not all search results are relevant or have correct information. Students should be encouraged to search until they can verify the validity of a source and determine if that source provides relevant information.

RESEARCH AND ASSESSMENTS

Document-based questions (DBQs) are an important assessment tool in history and social studies because they assess the student's reading comprehension, their comprehension of the unit's content, and their ability to analyze and apply information An effectively structured DBQ contains 3 – 15 primary and secondary source documents which all relate to a single question. The question should align with the objectives of the unit, and can even be the unit's essential question if one was used. The question should have multiple possible responses, and the documents should also provide evidence for a wide-range of responses.

While most often used with older students, DBQs can be adapted for younger learners as well by limiting the number and difficulty of documents used, providing clear and concrete questions, having students answer orally, or incorporating older students as aides in the writing process.

Independent research projects are another effective way to address students' analytical and interpretation abilities. In an independent research project, students should be directed to develop their own analytical question based on the larger objectives of the unit. They then will determine the types of sources they need to answer their question, read and interpret those resources, and finally use evidence from them to develop an argument, or thesis, in response to their question. The final presentation of their thesis and evidence can vary: a paper, an oral presentation, or a visual project. Independent research projects can range in length and depth depending on the content and the level of student. However, they should be incorporated into the length of a unit—not simply included at the end. By allowing students to select their own course of research, student engagement is also increased throughout the unit as a whole.

Simulations and debates are useful assessments to determine the students' ability to create knowledge. Like independent research projects, simulations and debates should be built into an entire unit, not just included at the end.

A **simulation** has students re-enact either an actual historical event—meeting or conference—or a fictional event that could realistically take place. Students are assigned to specific roles with specific and differing viewpoints. In assessing, the teacher should, in addition to the stated objectives of the unit, look for the student's ability to separate the perspective of their role from that of their own. This will show a high level of comprehension that extends beyond the simple facts of a situation.

TEACHING TIP

In debates, it can be useful to assign students to a position that is different from their personal one to deepen their understanding of all sides of an issue.

A **debate** can be structured around a pre-existing historical debate or a current, real-world issue related to the content. Students should be assigned to a particular side of the issue; they must conduct research into their topic and gather evidence specific to their assigned perspective.

Both simulations and debates can have a written component in addition to the oral presentation, and both should include a reflective component at the end in which students reflect on the issues addressed, their own comprehension, and their ability to convey the information and perspective effectively.

SAMPLE QUESTIONS

5) A teacher is planning a lesson on the election process based on an article about the most recent mayoral election. She first wants to determine quickly how well her students understood the article. Which of the following would be the most effective assessment to use?

A. Students create a drawing of the election process.

B. Students write a short biography about the current mayor.

C. The teacher has a one-on-one conference with each student to discuss the article.

D. Students write a new headline for the article.

Answer:

D. **Correct.** This would be a quick way to assess each student's understanding of the main idea of the article.

6) **Rebecca is teaching about the American Revolution. One objective of the unit is for students to understand the differing perspectives of colonists, the British government, and British citizens. Which of the following assessments would best measure that objective?**

A. a class-wide debate on whether the Revolution was avoidable

B. an independent research project on a particular colony's involvement in the lead up to the Revolution

C. a simulation of a fictional meeting between representatives of Parliament and the colonies

D. an essay test on the following question: Were the colonists right to revolt?

Answer:

C. **Correct.** The simulation between these groups would force students to examine the question of the Revolution from multiple angles.

Practice Test

WORLD HISTORY (30 QUESTIONS)

Directions: Read the question carefully and choose the best answer.

1

Despite the period of relative stability enjoyed by Europe during the High Middle Ages, the Black Death resulted in which of the following outcomes?

A. European powers were made vulnerable to attacks by the Magyars, who toppled the disorganized Holy Roman Empire.

B. Instability in Europe led to military conflict, division within the Catholic Church, and weakening of the Holy Roman Empire.

C. The Mongols were able to expand their empire into Eastern Europe.

D. Islamic powers were able to completely conquer the Iberian Peninsula as a result of instability there.

2

Following the collapse of the Western Roman Empire and the subsequent, disorganized "Dark Ages" in Europe,

A. the Catholic Church based in Rome lost power in Western Europe to the rising Greek Orthodox Church based in Constantinople.

B. the Byzantine Empire was able to conquer unorganized European land in what is today Germany.

C. Charlemagne united parts of Western and Central Europe—what would become the Holy Roman Empire—leading to a period of stability.

D. Charlemagne united parts of Western and Central Europe (including what would become France) under his rule, leading to a period of stability.

3

The Hittites were able to expand from Anatolia due to

A.   superior seafaring technology, allowing expansion into the Mediterranean.

B.   superior military technology, including chariots and weaponry.

C.   advanced technology imported from Greece.

D.   their development of bronze metallurgy.

4

During the Peloponnesian War,

A.   the dominant Hellenic powers, Crete and Sparta, went to war with each other.

B.   the dominant Hellenic powers, Athens and Sparta, went to war with the Ionian Greeks in Anatolia.

C.   Greece was able to unite as the dominant powers, Athens and Sparta, fought against Persia and the Ionian Greeks.

D.   the dominant Hellenic powers, Athens and Sparta, went to war with each other.

5

How did the Neolithic Era mark a major development in human evolution?

A.   the development of agriculture and beginning of settled societies

B.   the early use of the wheel

C.   the use of bronze to develop basic tools

D.   early medical treatment

6

During the Paleolithic Era,

A.   *Homo sapiens* was the only species of human in existence.

B.   multiple species of human existed.

C.   *Homo sapiens* likely eliminated all competition for resources.

D.   humans had not yet evolved.

7

There is evidence that the Bronze Age

A.   was a purely European phenomenon.

B.   only occurred in the Fertile Crescent.

C.   can be attributed to widespread sources of early bronze metallurgy.

D.   was a Chinese development.

8

Which of the following statements best explains the relevance of bronze metallurgy in early human civilizations?

A. Bronze technology allowed early societies in the Fertile Crescent to develop improved irrigation.

B. The Bronze Age gave rise to the Neolithic Era.

C. The development of bronze allowed humans to create copper.

D. Early civilizations like the Sumerians were able to use bronze for tools and weapons; geographic expansion and technological innovation (including in weaponry) resulted.

9

Many scholars argue that modern banking began in Venice in the fifteenth century. Which of the following strengthens this argument?

A. Venice was the first major colonial power, developing mercantilism.

B. Venice was a center of intellectual and cultural development.

C. Venice was a commercial center, ideally situated to profit from goods imported on the Silk Road and from Africa.

D. Venice was not badly affected by the plague.

10

One reason the Muslim Arabs were able to take over Byzantine- and Persian-controlled areas was

A. Muslims were ambivalent towards Christian minorities who may have opposed the Greek Orthodox Byzantines or the Zoroastrian Persians; these groups therefore preferred Arab-Muslim rule to more oppressive power structures.

B. Arabic-speaking people in the region were more responsive toward Arabic-speaking rulers.

C. Muslims already living in the Byzantine and Persian empires welcomed Islamic rule.

D. A and B only are correct.

11

While the Crusades enriched Europe in many ways, they did not

A. provide new learning to the west.

B. result in lasting land gains.

C. provide religious indulgences.

D. offer the opportunity to gain personal wealth.

12

How was Russia affected by the schism between Byzantine (Greek Orthodox) Christianity and the Roman Catholic Church?

A. Russia was unaffected.

B. Strong papal influences within Europe extended into Kiev and Russia, and Vladimir I converted to Catholicism, encouraging his subjects to do the same.

C. Byzantine missionaries moved north into Kiev and Russian territories; as a result, Vladimir I converted to Greek Orthodox Christianity and had his subjects do the same.

D. Disagreeing with the Catholic Church, Russia developed Eastern Orthodox Christianity and a separate Russian church.

13

Following the collapse of the Western Roman Empire, what was the status of serfs in Europe?

A. Serfs, while bound to the land on the manors where they lived and forced to farm for the lords, were not enslaved, nor were they forced to fight for lords; rather, they were to be protected.

B. Serfs were agricultural slaves expected to farm the land on manors in order to support lords.

C. Serfs were peasants on manors, expected to farm the land for lords but also able to farm their own land; they were free to leave manors if they wished but rarely did due to unsafe conditions.

D. Serfs were agricultural slaves who were also expected to fight for lords when called upon for defense.

14

What was a consequence of the decline of the Abbasid Caliphate?

I.   the dissolution of Islamic territories into lands dominated by various Islamic powers, including the Seljuks, the Mamluks, the Fatimids, and eventually the Ottoman Turks

II. a loss of connection with the Tang dynasty, a center of learning and technology

III. decentralization and disorganization in Central Asia, allowing for the rise of the Mongols and their subsequent empire

A. I, II, and III

B. I only

C. I and II only

D. I and III only

15

In approximately the same time period as Charlemagne's foundation of the Carolingian Empire, how did Central Europe become organized?

A.   The Catholic Church took power over a series of small states in Central Europe, organizing them as the Papal States.

B.   Charlemagne expanded his empire into Central Europe, organizing small states there as far east as modern-day Poland.

C.   Otto I became emperor of the Holy Roman Empire, a confederation of small states in Central Europe.

D.   Byzantine missionaries extended organized rule through the Balkans north into Central Europe, organizing the small states under the influence of the Greek Orthodox Church.

16

As head of the Catholic Church, the Pope was particularly influential because

A.   Catholicism had more followers than Greek Orthodox Christianity.

B.   the Pope held not only spiritual power, but also political power.

C.   the Church had special influence in Europe because it was based in Rome, a city of historical significance.

D.   the Pope had direct political control over most lords throughout feudal Europe.

17

The Kingdom of Mali developed due to

A.   its control over the trans-Saharan trade routes, enabling it to tax traders transporting goods between Morocco and the Atlantic coast.

B.   its ability to repel Islamic influences from the north.

C.   its control over gold and salt resources, generating tremendous wealth for the kingdom.

D.   its control over the trans-Saharan slave trade.

18

Which of the following statements describes both the French Revolution and the Russian Revolution?

A.   Both originated among the wealthiest elites.

B.   Both valued agricultural workers over the middle class.

C.   Both sought a totally egalitarian society, with publicly owned means of production.

D.   Both were based upon ideals articulated by intellectuals who were not members of the working or agricultural classes.

19

In South America, how was the Inca Empire able to consolidate its rule?

A. The Inca used strong military technology and tactics to subdue conquered peoples and expand their empire.

B. Driven by the belief in conversion, the Inca were able to convert Andean peoples to their own religion, gaining followers and therefore loyal subjects.

C. The Inca civilization had grown thanks to a surplus of maize and mastery of high altitude agriculture; due to their domestication of llamas and alpacas, the Inca were able to sustain their military with supplies to travel through the mountains.

D. Due to the mountainous terrain of the Andes, the Inca were unable to expand their empire far.

20

How did the United Kingdom reflect division in Europe and within Christianity in the seventeenth century?

A. Conflict between Protestants and Catholics over national leadership resulted in ongoing conflict and a series of unstable governments; however, following the Civil War, a Protestant monarchy was finally established in Great Britain and Ireland.

B. The purpose of the Glorious Revolution—to take back Protestant control of a Protestant country—was an example of the idea of the ethnic nation-state that was to take hold in Europe in later history.

C. Conflict between Protestants and Catholics over national leadership resulted in ongoing conflict and a series of unstable governments; however, following the Glorious Revolution, a Protestant monarchy was finally established.

D. While numerous Britons were Protestant, belonging to the Church of England, Puritans feared an overwhelming Catholic influence and left for the North American colonies to create a new church.

21

The system of mercantilism

A. enriched Spain by providing it with valuable raw materials, especially gold and silver.

B. placed particular value on merchants, allowing them to trade without taxes or duties.

C. was established in order to take advantage of the African slave trade.

D. was a market strategy to cut off trade between the Aztecs and other regional populations in the Western Hemisphere and Spain's European competitors like the Netherlands and Britain.

22

How did the Congress of Vienna affect the balance of power in Europe?

A. Prussia, the Austro-Hungarian Empire, France, Britain, and Russia agreed they would maintain that balance of power in Europe, following the Napoleonic Wars and setting a precedent for future European organization.

B. The Congress of Vienna marked the end of the imperial model in Europe; with the decline of the Holy Roman Empire, the last European empire had finally fallen.

C. Prussia, the Austro-Hungarian Empire, Britain, and Russia agreed on a series of sanctions against France following the Napoleonic Wars and French empire-building in Europe.

D. Prussia, Britain, and Russia emerged victorious, while France and the Austro-Hungarian Empire entered periods of decline.

23

Which of the following best describes the Counter-Reformation?

A. The Counter-Reformation was a response to corruption in the Church that divided the Catholic Church.

B. The Counter-Reformation was a response to the Protestant Reformation.

C. The Counter-Reformation occurred in response to the discovery of the Americas.

D. The Counter-Reformation occurred in response to the Enlightenment.

24

During the 1884 Berlin Conference, European imperial powers

A. established extraterritoriality within important Chinese cities to support their nationals who traded opium, silk, and other Chinese goods.

B. agreed upon spheres of influence whereby each European country would dominate different parts of China.

C. determined which parts of Africa would be controlled by which European powers, a process also called the "scramble for Africa."

D. established the Triple Alliance and the Triple Entente, setting the stage for the system of alliances that would eventually spark the First World War.

25

Which of the following best describes the Warsaw Pact?

A. a defense agreement between the Soviet Union and Eastern Bloc

B. a Soviet alliance with Poland

C. Soviet control over Eastern Europe

D. the division of Eastern Europe after WWII

26

Choose the best description for the Russian strategy of empire-building.

A. Russia focused on colonizing overseas, strengthening its navy to build a trans-oceanic empire.

B. Russia focused on overland expansion, moving eastward into northern Asia across Siberia and westward into Eastern Europe.

C. Russia remained isolated, avoiding expansion and focusing on industrialization instead.

D. Russia lacked the resources to build an empire and struggled to maintain its agrarian-based society.

27

How were European empires affected by nationalism in the eighteenth and nineteenth centuries?

A. European empires like the Austro-Hungarian Empire benefitted from nationalism, as Austrians and Hungarians were more loyal to the imperial government.

B. The Austro-Hungarian Empire lost its Balkan territories to the Ottoman Empire, which was perceived to be more tolerant of Muslim minorities.

C. Given the nature of empire—consolidated rule over an extended region home to diverse peoples—nationalism threatened empire as ethnic groups began to advocate for representation in imperial government.

D. Given the nature of empire—consolidated rule over an extended region home to diverse peoples—nationalism threatened empire as ethnic groups began to advocate for their own independent states.

28

Slaves were originally brought to the Americas as part of the triangular trade in order to do what?

A. work on cotton plantations

B. work on sugar plantations

C. work in colonists' homes

D. all of the above

29

The Meiji Restoration was

A.   a Japanese attempt to restore traditional Japan and reinvigorate Japanese culture as it had been before Western incursions into the country.

B.   a period of modernization and westernization in Japan.

C.   the early stage of Japanese imperialism in Asia, when it invaded Korea.

D.   a cultural movement in Japan to restore Shintoism and traditional poetry.

30

Following the collapse of the Ottoman Empire after the First World War, European countries took control of the Middle East, establishing protectorates according to arbitrary boundaries and installing rulers in accordance with European strategic interests. What effect has this had on the Middle East in the twentieth and twenty-first centuries?

A.   The Middle East has not been greatly affected.

B.   Illegitimate national borders and rulers have led to instability in the region.

C.   Improved governance, thanks to the protectorates, and improved stability following the decline of the Ottoman Empire in the region.

D.   European investment in strategic resources supported long-term political stability in the Middle East.

US History (36 questions)

Directions: Read the question carefully and choose the best answer.

1

What advantage did the colonists have in the American Revolution?

A.   vast financial wealth

B.   superior weaponry

C.   strong leadership and knowledge of the terrain

D.   a professional military and access to mercenaries

2

How did the views of the Federalists and the Anti-Federalists differ during the Constitutional Convention?

A.   The views of the Federalists and Anti-Federalists did not significantly differ at the Constitutional Convention.

B.   The Anti-Federalists did not believe in a Constitution at all, while the Federalists insisted on including the Bill of Rights.

C.   The Anti-Federalists favored a stronger Constitution and federal government, while Federalists were concerned that states would risk losing their autonomy.

D.   The Federalists favored a stronger Constitution and federal government, while Anti-Federalists were concerned that states would risk losing their autonomy.

3

Which of the following best describes the conditions faced by Latinos and Latinas who had remained in western territories won by the United States in the Mexican-American War?

A.   They were treated with derision; many lost land and wealth they had held under Mexico, and did not enjoy the same rights under the law as citizens, even though they had been promised American citizenship in the Treaty of Guadalupe Hidalgo.

B.   While many had lost land and wealth they had held under Mexico, they were entitled to and received restitution from the government of the United States.

C.   They were treated equally in social and political situations under the United States.

D.   Most Latinos and Latinas left the western territories for Mexico following the Mexican-American War, due to discriminatory conditions they faced under the United States government.

4

Why was the Mayflower Compact an important contribution to the foundation of American government?

A.   It provided for equal treatment of all Christians under the law.

B.   It was the first treaty between European settlers (the Pilgrims) and Native Americans.

C.   It laid out terms for government with the consent of the governed.

D.   It allowed people of all faiths to practice their religions freely under the law.

5

What was one reason for the election of Andrew Jackson?

A.   Jackson was able to find a solution to the first Nullification Crisis.

B.   Allowing those white males who did not own property to vote was a boon to Jackson, who was popular with the "common man."

C.   Jackson's popularity with landowners in Northern states guaranteed him the funds he needed to win the presidency.

D.   Jackson and his vice president, John C. Calhoun, were a strong and popular team when running for election.

6

What did the Compromise of 1850 accomplish?

A.   It admitted California and Maine as free states and strengthened the Fugitive Slave Act.

B.   It admitted California as a free state, Utah and New Mexico with slavery to be decided by popular sovereignty, and strengthened the Fugitive Slave Act.

C.   It admitted California, Utah, and New Mexico as free states, and strengthened the Fugitive Slave Act.

D.   It admitted California, Utah, and New Mexico as states with slavery to be decided by popular sovereignty, and strengthened the Fugitive Slave Act.

7

What was a consequence of the Kansas-Nebraska Act?

A.   the Fugitive Slave Act

B.   the Compromise of 1850

C.   violence between pro- and anti-slavery advocates in Kansas over the legalization of slavery ("Bleeding Kansas")

D.   the Missouri Compromise

8

In the Emancipation Proclamation, President Lincoln declared an end to slavery

A.   in Kentucky and Missouri.

B.   in the Union only.

C.   in slave states that had not seceded from the Union.

D.   in the rebel states.

9

What assets did the Confederacy have during the Civil War?

A.   The Confederacy had superior weaponry and production resources.

B.   The Confederacy maintained brisk trade with Europe, enabling it to fund the war.

C.   The Confederacy benefitted from strong military leadership and high morale among the population.

D.   The Confederacy's strong infrastructure allowed it to transport supplies and people efficiently throughout the South.

10

Following the Civil War, the United States ratified the Thirteenth, Fourteenth, and Fifteenth Amendments to the Constitution. What did these amendments guarantee?

A.   an end to slavery, equal rights for all Americans, and voting rights for all Americans, respectively

B.   an end to slavery, equal rights for all Americans, and voting rights for all African Americans, respectively

C.   an end to slavery, equal rights for all American men, and voting rights for all African American men, respectively

D.   an end to slavery, equal rights for Americans, and voting rights for African American men, respectively

11

The Sioux War

A.   was instigated by the United States, which wanted to take back land it had granted to the Sioux.

B.   resulted in a very bloody battle in which the United States was defeated; however the US eventually took the land from the Sioux.

C.   was an example of unity among western tribes.

D.   all of the above

12

Crafted by President Lincoln, the Ten Percent Plan

A. called for the rebel states to pay 10 percent of the costs of the war in restitution to the North as a condition of readmission to the Union.

B. ensured that African Americans would be represented by at least 10 percent of Congress following the Civil War.

C. re-admitted any rebel state to the Union once at least 10 percent of its citizens swore allegiance to the Union.

D. required 10 percent of the population of a rebel state to move to the North before it would be re-admitted to the Union.

13

The Interstate Commerce Act and the Sherman Antitrust Act

A. immediately went into effect to regulate the railroad industry and break up monopolies.

B. remained largely toothless until the First World War.

C. remained largely toothless until the administration of Theodore Roosevelt.

D. immediately went into effect to promote congressional efforts to regulate interstate commerce.

14

The Spanish-American War

A. brought the United States territories in Asia, the Pacific Ocean, and the Caribbean.

B. was triggered in part by public support generated by sensationalist yellow journalism.

C. could be viewed as a precursor to Theodore Roosevelt's Roosevelt Corollary to the Monroe Doctrine.

D. all of the above

15

Women did not receive full suffrage in the United States until which of the following?

A. The Seneca Falls Convention was held.

B. The Nineteenth Amendment was ratified.

C. The Equal Rights Amendment was ratified.

D. The Voting Rights Act of 1965 was passed.

16

Nineteenth-century workers organized labor unions for all of the following reasons except for which of the following?

A.   they were not paid fairly for their work

B.   their shifts were frequently 12 – 14 hours a day

C.   to overthrow capitalists like Carnegie and Rockefeller

D.   dangerous work conditions

17

Within the two years following WWI, the United States would

A.   join the League of Nations.

B.   join NATO.

C.   ratify the Treaty of Versailles.

D.   none of the above

18

During FDR's terms in office, which of the following was created?

A.   Medicare

B.   Social Security

C.   the Federal Reserve

D.   all of the above

19

By signing the Atlantic Charter, the United States and Great Britain

A.   agreed to divide the world into democratic capitalist and communist regions.

B.   decided to jointly occupy Europe indefinitely.

C.   established the Atlantic Ocean as a neutral area.

D.   agreed on a postwar world characterized by free trade and self-determination.

20

Which of the following Cold War events is an example of the US foreign policy of containment, in the spirit of the Truman Doctrine, put into effect?

A.   the Cuban Missile Crisis

B.   the Korean War

C.   *glasnost* and *perestroika*

D.   the Non-Aligned Movement

21

Johnson's vision of a Great Society

A.   included programs to stabilize the economy and promote civil rights, like Social Security.

B.   included programs as part of the War on Poverty to support the disadvantaged, like Medicare, Head Start, and the Department of Housing and Urban Development.

C.   included programs to strengthen society in the face of communism, like the CIA and the Department of Homeland Security.

D.   included a plan to end the war in Vietnam.

22

How did feminist advocacy groups effect empowering change for women in the United States?

A.   They obtained ratification of an Equal Rights Amendment to the Constitution guaranteeing equal rights for men and women in public places and affairs in the United States.

B.   They advocated for the passage of the Equal Pay Act, which ensured that men and women would be paid equally for equal work done in the same workplace.

C.   They supported Supreme Court cases that ensured women would receive certain health benefits throughout the United States.

D.   B and C only

23

What was the relevance of the Gulf of Tonkin Resolution?

A.   It gave Congress the power to declare war against the North Vietnamese forces.

B.   It authorized the president to take military action against North Vietnamese forces.

C.   It authorized the military to take action against North Vietnamese forces.

D.   It authorized the president to take military action against South Vietnamese forces.

24

The Civil Rights Act of 1964

A.   struck down restrictions on voting rights for African Americans.

B.   guaranteed equal rights for all Americans, regardless of their race, gender, religion, or sexual orientation.

C.   ended segregation.

D.   all of the above

25

In which of the following international conflicts of the 1990s did the United States play a major role in peacemaking?

I. the war in Bosnia

II. the Rwandan Civil War

III. the conflict in Northern Ireland

A. I only

B. I and II

C. I and III

D. I, II and III

26

In 2008, a period of economic stagnation in the United States known as the Great Recession began. What was one important cause of this crisis?

A. the extension of high-risk car loans to borrowers, who were unable to pay back their car loans, resulting in abandoned cars throughout the United States, delinquency, and broader financial consequences

B) the extension of high-interest loans and mortgages to high-risk borrowers who were unable to pay off their mortgages, resulting in defaults, and foreclosure with broader financial consequences

C. the extension of student loans to borrowers who were unable to find jobs and therefore unable to repay the loans, resulting in forbearance, delinquency, and defaults with broader financial consequences

D. the extension of high-interest credit cards to high-risk borrowers who were then unable to keep up with payments, resulting in delinquency and defaults with broader financial consequences

27

NAFTA accomplished which of the following?

A. opened borders between the United States, Canada, and Mexico, allowing for free movement of goods and people between these three countries

B. initiated free trade between the United States, Mexico, and Canada, facilitating and strengthening trade between these three countries

C. created a union similar to the European Union in North America, in which Canada, Mexico, and the United States shared similar policy goals and consulted each other on matters of shared concern

D. established common immigration procedures between Mexico, the United States, and Canada

28

A consequence of Operation Desert Storm, or the Gulf War of 1991, was

A.   the occupation of Iraq by the United States.

B.   the occupation of Kuwait by Iraq.

C.   the de facto establishment of the United States as the world's sole superpower in the wake of the fall of the Soviet Union.

D.   improved cooperation in the United Nations between the United States and the former Soviet Union, now represented by the Russian Federation.

29

The Iranian hostage crisis

A.   resulted in the establishment of an anti-American theocracy in Iran.

B.   contributed to the election of Ronald Reagan to the presidency, which led to the escalation of weapons production and the arms race.

C.   resulted in regional instability, forcing the Soviet invasion of Afghanistan.

D.   contributed to the election of Jimmy Carter to the presidency, which led to a period of détente with the Soviet Union.

30

The Cuban Missile Crisis ultimately resulted in

A.   the installation of the Castro regime.

B.   the fall of the Castro regime.

C.   a new opening of dialogue between the United States and the Soviet Union.

D.   the end of a period of détente between the United States and the Soviet Union.

31

The United States invaded Afghanistan following the terrorist attacks of September 11, 2001

A.   in order to defeat the Taliban, who had attacked the United States.

B.   in order to capture Osama bin Laden and al Qaeda, who had attacked the United States and who were harbored by the Taliban, the government of Afghanistan.

C.   in order to defeat al Qaeda, the government of Afghanistan.

D.   in order to defeat al Qaeda, which held weapons of mass destruction in Afghanistan.

Read the excerpt and answer questions 32 and 33.

It is not true that the United States feels any land hunger or entertains any projects as regards the other nations of the Western Hemisphere save such as are for their welfare. All that this country desires is to see the neighboring countries stable, orderly, and prosperous. Any country whose people conduct themselves well can count upon our hearty friendship. If a nation shows that it knows how to act with reasonable efficiency and decency in social and political matters, if it keeps order and pays its obligations, it need fear no interference from the United States. Chronic wrongdoing, or an impotence which results in a general loosening of the ties of civilized society, may in America, as elsewhere, ultimately require intervention by some civilized nation, and in the Western Hemisphere the adherence of the United States to the Monroe Doctrine may force the United States, however reluctantly, in flagrant cases of such wrongdoing or impotence, to the exercise of an international police power.

Theodore Roosevelt's Annual Message to
Congress, December 6, 1904 (*Roosevelt
Corollary to the Monroe Doctrine*)

32

What is Roosevelt saying about United States' intentions in the Western Hemisphere?

A. The United States will not intervene in domestic matters in Latin American countries.

B. The United States will only intervene in domestic matters in Latin American countries upon request.

C. The United States will intervene in Latin American countries when it sees fit.

D. The United States will intervene in Latin American countries when it sees fit, and may use force.

33

According to the Monroe Doctrine, the United States would view European interference in Latin America as a sign of aggression, consolidating US influence in that region. What is different about the Roosevelt Corollary to the Monroe Doctrine?

A. It stationed US troops throughout Latin America.

B. It strengthened commercial ties between the United States and Latin American countries.

C. It limited diplomatic relations between Europe and Latin America.

D. It provided for US military intervention in Latin America.

34

Segregation was found unconstitutional by which of the following Supreme Court decisions?

A.   *Brown v. Board of Education*

B.   *Plessy v. Ferguson*

C.   *Scott v. Sanford*

D.   *Korematsu v. US*

35

Which of the following is a hallmark of conservative ideology?

A.   open borders to facilitate international trade

B.   low taxes

C.   labor rights

D.   a small, efficient military

36

Which of the following US actions contributed to the fall of the Soviet Union?

I.   the "arms race"—high extensive military spending and weapons development in the 1980s

II.   arming anti-Soviet proxies in Afghanistan—the mujahedeen

III. supporting Boris Yeltsin in the coup against Mikhail Gorbachev

A.   I and II

B.   I and III

C.   II and III

D.   I, II, and III

TEXAS HISTORY (20 QUESTIONS)

Directions: Read the question carefully and choose the best answer.

1

The first Texans to make contact with Europeans were

A. the Apache.

B. the Karankawa.

C. the Caddo.

D. the Comanche.

2

The driving force behind Spanish exploration and settlement of Texas was

A. to convert native Texans to Christianity.

B. to capture land to raise cattle, a profitable good to satisfy demand for beef in Europe.

C. to create a buffer zone to prevent French incursions into Mexico.

D. to pursue rumors of gold farther inland in Texas.

3

Which of the following best explains why the Spanish were threatened by French exploration southwest into Texas?

A. France had allied with the Karankawa in order to drive the Spanish from Texas.

B. French exploration southwest from the Great Lakes and Quebec into the Mississippi region threatened Spain's dominance of the North American continent.

C. French exploration southwest from the Great Lakes and Quebec toward Texas was a potential threat to the Spanish empire in the Americas.

D. France showed interest in taking control over Texas' considerable gold and silver resources.

4

Filibuster settlers

A. were settlers from Mexico who sought to prevent Anglo settlement in Texas.

B. legally came from the United States in search of land and economic opportunity.

C. were whites (Anglos) who illegally immigrated to Texas seeking land and economic opportunity.

D. were invited by Galvez and Bouligny to settle in Texas.

5

At the Convention of 1833, Texans drew up a resolution demanding

A.   an end to restrictions on slavery in Texas.

B.   separation from Coahuila.

C.   more protection from the Apaches and Comanche.

D.   all of the above

6

Why was early resistance disorganized in the Texas Revolution?

A.   Even though Sam Houston was chosen to lead an army, James Bowie and James Fannin were already leading uprisings, making it difficult to consolidate military power against Mexico.

B.   Texans were reluctant to unite under Sam Houston's leadership because he had been governor of Tennessee.

C.   Infighting between Sam Houston and Stephen F. Austin threatened unity among Texas' leaders.

D.   Sam Houston and David Crockett, both formerly of Tennessee, were unable to win the loyalty of people born in Texas who were needed to serve in a military capacity.

7

How did the Republic of Texas raise income?

A.   printing money

B.   selling the rights to Galveston

C.   attracting settlers with land and land scrip

D.   investing in infrastructure

8

Which of the following best describes the changing relationships between Anglos and Tejanos in the Republic of Texas?

A.   Anglos and Tejanos were able to work together as equals in the Republic of Texas, since they enjoyed equal rights under the law.

B.   Tejanos were forced out of Texas to Mexico by Anglo-American immigrants.

C.   Tejanos maintained strong economic ties to Mexico, while Anglos had stronger trading links with the United States; the two groups did not interact economically in Texas.

D.   Even though Tejano men were Texas citizens, increasing numbers of Anglo-American immigrants saw them as Mexican agents and they lived as second-class citizens, increasing ethnic tensions in Texas.

9

How were Texas' current borders finalized?

A. Texas claimed land won by the United States in the Mexican-American War.

B. Texas retained the same borders it had been assigned when it was part of Mexico.

C. Texas accepted its present-day borders as part of the Compromise of 1850.

D. Texas' borders were drawn following the Civil War and the dissolution of the Confederacy.

10

In 1861, the Secession Convention wrote a new constitution. What was one of its stipulations?

A. special protection for minorities of Czech and German descent

B. the legality of slavery

C. special protection for Tejanos under the Confederacy

D. Texan independence

11

The Constitution of 1868

A. was written by Democrats who wanted to undo the changes made by Republicans, many of whom came from outside Texas, to Texan law.

B. decentralized government, weakening the state legislature.

C. is still Texas' constitution today.

D. was written by Republicans during Reconstruction, strengthening state government.

12

Which of the following best explains the decline of the cattle drive?

A. Violence in northern Texas from Great Plains tribes prevented ranchers from driving cattle north to Kansas for transport on railroads to population centers in the east.

B. The development of north-south railroads in Texas made it unnecessary to drive cattle north to meet intercontinental railroad lines.

C. Ranching declined in Texas as settlement increased in Montana and Wyoming, where developments like the Matador Ranch proved the practice was more profitable.

D. Laborers left jobs as cowboys for work in the growing urban areas of Dallas and Houston.

13

The Redeemers

A. had supported the Confederacy.

B. were opposed to Radical Republican intervention in Texas.

C. tended to be Democrats.

D. all of the above

14

In the nineteenth century, one of Texas' major products was cotton. What was the impact of the cotton industry in Texas on African Americans following the Civil War?

A. Many African Americans began their own cotton plantations in Central Texas, thanks to the support provided by the Freedmen's Bureau.

B. Enslaved African Americans who had worked on Texas plantations were granted special protection under the Constitution of 1876 and given parcels of land to farm.

C. Formerly enslaved African Americans were expelled from Central Texas to prevent them from becoming successful cotton farmers.

D. Many formerly enslaved African Americans became sharecroppers—often on the same land where they had been enslaved—remaining trapped in an exploitative system.

15

State Attorney General and Governor Jim Hogg was popular due to which of the following actions?

A. He introduced legislation in Congress creating the Interstate Commerce Commission.

B. He prosecuted railroads that wanted to limit or halt service to small, isolated towns.

C. He sued insurance companies that did not meet their obligations.

D. B and C only

16

Which of the following explains Governor James Ferguson's popularity?

A. his promises to subsidize cotton farmers

B. his support for Texas financial interests thanks to his roots in banking

C. his support for the rural poor and improvements in infrastructure and education

D. his vows to abolish the Texas Railroad Commission

17

How did the political leader Henry B. Gonzalez advocate for civil rights in Texas?

A.   He sponsored legislation to desegregate San Antonio parks.

B.   He fought state legislation to re-segregate Texas schools.

C.   He filibustered state efforts to circumvent federal civil rights legislation.

D.   all of the above

18

Barbara Jordan, the US representative and first African American Texas state senator

A.   worked in the State Senate for the creation of the Fair Employment Practices Commission.

B.   played an important role in the Watergate hearings as a congresswoman representing Texas.

C.   represented Texas in the US Senate for several terms.

D.   A and B only

19

What was the impact of the Middle East oil embargo on Texas during the 1970s?

A.   The Texas economy suffered as those in the oil industry lost their jobs.

B.   The Texas petroleum industry grew rapidly to meet the demand for oil in the United States, which could not obtain it from the Middle East.

C.   Drop in demand for oil led to diversification into natural gas.

D.   Wind power became an important energy source in Texas thanks to its open plains and empty spaces.

20

In the early twenty-first century, how has Texas' population changed?

A.   Hispanic and African American populations are growing.

B.   Hispanic and African American populations are shrinking.

C.   More people are moving to rural areas.

D.   More people are leaving Texas than ever before.

SOCIAL STUDIES FOUNDATIONS, SKILLS, RESEARCH, AND INSTRUCTION (14 QUESTIONS)

Directions: Read the question carefully and choose the best answer.

1

A map of an ancient empire would be most useful for the study of

A.   geography.

B.   history.

C.   political science.

D.   anthropology.

2

What exercise would be most helpful for an economics teacher to assign to students?

A.   a writing project

B.   a group exercise

C.   an assignment to create graphs relative to provided data

D.   a research project about an important economist

3

Why are primary sources important for historians?

A.   Primary sources provide strong information about relevant time periods and strong evidence in historical argument.

B.   Primary sources are useful in historical research, but are not any more useful than secondary or tertiary sources.

C.   There is no difference between a primary and secondary source.

D.   Historians do not use primary sources.

4

Which of the following lessons helps students develop an understanding of a market economy?

A.   Students explore economic competition in their area and identify local business competitors.

B.   Students explore making smart buying decisions by comparing prices of goods.

C.   Students work together to decide what is necessary to rebuild a community.

D.   Students explore how individuals generate income.

5

A credible anthropologist would conduct research

A.   on the internet.

B.   in the library.

C.   in the field.

D.   on the phone.

6

Geography

A.   is the study of maps.

B.   is the study of the earth.

C.   is the study of how agriculture affects the earth.

D.   is the study of space and how people affect and are affected by the physical space they inhabit.

7

Half of a class does not understand the concept of supply and demand. Which of the following lessons would be the most appropriate to re-teach this concept?

A.   asking students to study varied economics-related vocabulary for a mid-unit test

B.   teaching the same lesson students were initially exposed to

C.   rephrasing the definition of supply and demand, then providing students with different examples and restating why the laws of supply and demand are important to economics

D.   moving on to another concept and hoping that repeated exposure to the words will help the students gain an understanding of the issue

8

Which of the following graphic organizers would help students compare and contrast Greek and Roman culture?

A.   a KWL chart

B.   a spider map

C.   a tally chart

D.   a Venn diagram

9

Which of the following would be best assessed using an analytic rubric?

A. the overall quality of a student's assignment

B. appropriate use of vocabulary in an assignment

C. a student's understanding of the causes and consequences of the major battles of World War I

D. student performance based on a student's understanding of the aftermath of World War I and its influence on World War II

10

Which of the following describes the most appropriate method for assessing a student's knowledge of the names and dates of major battles of the Civil War?

A. a multiple-choice test

B. a research report

C. a debate

D. a portfolio

11

Which of the following would be the most appropriate question for students to consider in preparing a debate on industrialization?

A. What were the major inventions of the Industrial Revolution?

B. Which invention created during the Industrial Revolution influenced society the most?

C. Why did the Industrial Revolution happen?

D. What factors contributed to poor living conditions for workers during the Industrial Revolution?

12

Which of the following is true when teaching students to evaluate sources?

A. Students should only consider internet sources.

B. Students need to determine the credibility and contemporaneity of the source.

C. Students should only look at secondary sources.

D. Students can include biased resources in their research.

13

Which of the following would be the most appropriate lesson for teaching the concept of communication?

A.   studying the impact of bullying in school

B.   studying how communities use transportation to move from place to place

C.   studying the reasons for migration

D.   studying how leaders are elected in the United States

14

Which of the following would be the most effective method to teach students about voting?

A.   Students read a book about the drafting of the US Constitution.

B.   Students read a document about antipathy in the South towards the Union during the Reconstruction period.

C.   Students learn about why a president can only serve for two terms.

D.   Students follow news about the current presidential election and discuss the importance of developing an informed opinion on each candidate.

Answer Key

WORLD HISTORY

1)

B. The continental—indeed, global—impact of the Black Death destabilized much of Europe.

2)

D. Charlemagne was Frankish and stabilized parts of Western and Central Europe; most of the Carolingian Empire eventually became France.

3)

B. The Hittites were skilled charioteers and were early pioneers of iron weaponry.

4)

D. The Peloponnesian War was between the major Greek powers.

5)

A. Developing agricultural practices in the Neolithic Era allowed humans to establish settled societies sustained by reliable food sources.

6)

B. During the Paleolithic Era, hominids like *Australopithecus* and later, *Homo habilis*, *Homo erectus*, *Homo neanderthalensis* lived.

7)

C. Humans began using bronze globally and concurrently.

8)

D. Bronze improved weapons and tools; improved weaponry meant expanded control over territory and more secure societies that could continue to develop.

9)

C. As a commercial center and well-situated to handle goods arriving in Europe from the Silk Road and from Africa, Venice developed banking institutions that influenced modern banking.

10)

D. Even though the peoples living under Byzantine and Persian rule were not

Muslim or Arab, the Islamic tradition of tolerance toward the "People of the Book" and, to an extent, Zoroastrians, made them more acceptable rulers than the oppressive and disorganized collapsing regimes; furthermore, many people in the region spoke Arabic, which made it easier to accept Arab rule.

11)

B.   European powers controlled some areas in the Levant, but only temporarily.

12)

C.   Byzantine missionaries spread Orthodox Christianity north; Vladimir I converted and a tradition of Orthodox Christianity took root in Russia and Ukraine.

13)

A.   Serfs were not slaves, but they were not entirely free as they were bound to the lord's land and had to farm it. However, the lord was obligated to protect them and they were not expected to fight.

14)

A.   Various powers controlled Egypt and Southwest Asia, until the Ottoman Empire took control of the region. Connection with China dissipated as the Silk Road fell out of use and the Mongol invasions destabilized Central Asia.

15)

C.   Central Europe became organized into the Holy Roman Empire for several hundred years, beginning under Otto I.

16)

B.   At the time, the Pope controlled the Papal States in Italy, which were political territories; furthermore, he

was extremely influential among European leaders.

17)

C.   Mali became wealthy due to gold and salt, valuable natural resources.

18)

D.   While the peasantry revolted in the countryside and the people stormed the Bastille in 1789, the French Revolution was based on the Enlightenment ideals embodied in the Declaration of the Rights of Man and Citizen issued by the National Constituent Assembly dominated by the Bourgeoisie of the Third Estate. Likewise, the Russian Revolution was instigated by Lenin and Trotsky, urban intellectuals inspired by the socialism of Karl Marx. Lenin and Trotsky helped organize the proletariat in a communist revolution overthrowing the tsar.

19)

C.   Agricultural surplus and advanced transportation in high altitude terrain enabled the Inca military to range widely throughout the Andes.

20)

C.   The Glorious Revolution, in which the Protestants William and Mary deposed the Catholic James II, secured a future of Protestant monarchies in Britain.

21)

A.   Mercantilism enriched colonial powers at the expense of colonies, increasing their power relative to other European countries.

22)

A.   European countries agreed to affirm their territories and respect sovereignty to stabilize Europe.

23)

B. The Counter-Reformation re-converted Protestants back to Catholicism, spread Catholic education, and fought heresy.

24)

C. The 1884 Berlin Conference determined the division of Africa into colonies between the European imperial powers. This was done without regard for or consultation with Africans.

25)

A. The Warsaw Pact was a mutual defense agreement between Eastern European countries and the USSR in response to NATO.

26)

B. Russia expanded to the east, taking control of Siberia. Russia also extended westward to an extent, controlling part of Eastern Europe.

27)

D. Nationalism triggered independence movements and advocacy.

28)

D. Slaves were forced to do all of the above work—and more.

29)

B. The Meiji Restoration was a period of industrialization and westernization in Japan.

30)

B. Borders did not take into account history or ethnic groups; rulers installed did not necessarily have legitimacy in the eyes of the people, leading to political instability and violence.

US HISTORY

1)

C. The colonial military did have strong leaders, and an intimate knowledge of the terrain, many having been born there.

2)

D. The Federalists were the driving force behind a stronger Constitution that would empower the United States federal government; the Anti-Federalists worked to protect state sovereignty and ensured the passage of the Bill of Rights to protect certain rights not explicitly guaranteed in the Constitution itself.

3)

A. Hispanic residents of the land the United States gained in the Treaty of Guadalupe Hidalgo did not obtain all they were promised; in fact, many lost their property and were not treated equally under the law or in society.

4)

C. As a governing document, the Mayflower Compact was notable in that it provided for governance with the consent of the governed, a departure from British rule.

5)

B. Jackson was extremely popular among the lower classes and rural farmers of the South; changing voting laws to allow dispossessed white males to vote expanded the electorate, giving him a huge advantage.

6)

B. The Compromise of 1850 admitted California as a free state; however it strengthened the Fugitive Slave Act. The legalization of slavery in Utah and New Mexico would be decided by the voters.

7)

C. Violence broke out over the question of legalizing slavery in Kansas, where it had previously been prohibited.

8)

D. The Emancipation Proclamation freed the slaves in the Confederacy.

9)

C. The Confederacy had excellent military leaders; many Confederate leaders and much of the population strongly believed in the right of states to make decisions without federal interference, not only about slavery but also about trade and other issues.

10)

D. The Thirteenth Amendment abolished slavery; the Fourteenth Amendment promised equal protection under the law to all U.S. citizens; the Fifteenth Amendment ensured that (male) African Americans and former slaves could vote.

11)

D. All of the choices are true.

12)

C. The Ten Percent Plan reunited the country by allowing states to rejoin the Union with only 10 percent of their populations swearing allegiance to it.

13)

C.   It was not until Theodore Roosevelt came into office that these acts were effectively used for their intended purpose: to create a fair market in the United States by eliminating trusts and monopolies.

14)

D.   All of the answer choices are true.

15)

B.   The Nineteenth Amendment allowed women to vote; it was ratified in 1920.

16)

C.   Labor unions sought improved working conditions, not the overthrow of capitalism.

17)

D.   None of the choices are true.

18)

B.   The Social Security Act was part of the New Deal.

19)

D.   The Atlantic Charter embodied the shared vision of the United States and Great Britain for the postwar world.

20)

B.   The United States fought North Korean, Soviet- and Chinese-supported communists in Korea, preventing them from establishing an entirely communist Korea and establishing a capitalist, western-allied South Korea.

21)

B.   The Great Society was rooted in Johnson's War on Poverty and in liberalism: the belief that government programs should support those in need (and that the U.S. should be active in fighting communism overseas).

22)

D.   B and C are correct.

23)

B.   The Gulf of Tonkin Resolution gave the president power to commit military troops in Vietnam without Congressional authorization.

24)

C.   The Civil Rights Act of 1964 made segregation illegal.

25)

C.   The United States led peace talks to resolve conflict in Bosnia and the former Yugoslavia as well as in Northern Ireland.

26)

B.   The Subprime Mortgage Crisis was a central cause of the Great Recession.

27)

B.   NAFTA is a free trade agreement among the three countries.

28)

C.   Having led the coalition that defeated Iraq in the 1991 Gulf War, the United States proved its position as the sole superpower following the end of the Cold War with the collapse of the Soviet Union.

29)

B.   President Carter's inability to resolve the crisis helped propel Ronald Reagan to victory in the 1980 presidential election; Reagan took an aggressive stance against the Soviet

Union and escalated the arms race, intensifying the Cold War throughout the 1980s.

30)

C. Following the extreme tensions between the two countries, the United States and the Soviet Union improved dialogue in the early 1960s, leading to a period of détente.

31)

B. Neutralizing Osama bin Laden and his network—al Qaeda—was the stated objective for the invasion of Afghanistan.

32)

D. Roosevelt states that the United States will intervene in Latin America when it deems it necessary, and will use force if needed.

33)

D. According to the Roosevelt Corollary to the Monroe Doctrine, the United

States would intervene militarily in Latin America if it felt that its interests were threatened.

34)

A. *Brown v. Board of Education* found that keeping races separate (in this case, in segregated schools) could not ensure that all people would receive equal treatment, and that segregation was therefore unconstitutional.

35)

B. Conservatives believe in low taxes to boost business.

36)

A. The United States outspent the Soviet Union in military and weapons, helping precipitate its fall. US support for anti-Soviet fighters in Afghanistan also weakened the Soviet Union.

TEXAS HISTORY

1)

   B. Cabeza de Vaca encountered the Karankawa on the Gulf Coast in the early sixteenth century; the Karankawa were fishers and hunter-gatherers along the coastline.

2)

   D. Early Spanish expeditions in Texas were driven by the search for gold.

3)

   C. Texas was a useful buffer zone, protecting Mexico and the rest of the Spanish empire in the Americas from French and British interests in North America. A threat to Texas represented a potential threat to the empire.

4)

   C. Filibuster settlers were white settlers who illegally came to Texas in search of opportunity.

5)

   D. All of the answer choices are true.

6)

   A. Widespread uprisings made it difficult for Houston to consolidate one army.

7)

   C. Rich in land, Texas attracted settlers who would contribute to economic development.

8)

   D. Tejanos were viewed with suspicion by Anglos, particularly Anglo-American immigrants. Despite their legal standing, Tejanos lived as second-class citizens.

9)

   C. In exchange for giving up claims to land that would become New Mexico and for $10 million, Texas accepted its present-day borders as part of the Compromise of 1850.

10)

   B. The new constitution specifically affirmed the legality of slavery in Texas.

11)

   D. The Constitution of 1868 was written by Republicans during Reconstruction. It strengthened state government; it also represented what Democrats felt to be interference and overreach by "carpetbaggers" and Radical Republicans.

12)

   B. The first major north-south railroad was built through Dallas; there was no need to drive cattle north as they could be transported by rail.

13)

   D. Redeemers were generally Democrats who had supported the Confederacy and worked against Republican intervention. All of the above are correct.

14)

   D. Central Texas cotton production relied on sharecropping.

15)

   D. Both answer choices B and C are correct. Hogg prosecuted railroads and insurance companies.

16)

C. Ferguson campaigned in rural areas and presided over improvements in infrastructure and education (in addition to scandal).

17)

D. All of the choices are true.

18)

D. Both answer choices A and B are true.

19)

B. Texas became a major source for petroleum, boosting the state's economy and enriching many Texans in the energy industry.

20)

A. Since the 1990s, Hispanic and African American populations in Texas have been growing, especially in urban areas.

SOCIAL STUDIES FOUNDATIONS, SKILLS, RESEARCH, AND INSTRUCTION

1)

B. A historian would likely find such a map useful in order to visualize the breadth of a certain empire.

2)

C. Getting practice creating the graphs reflective of economic concepts using data provided by the instructor will help economics students better grasp economics concepts.

3)

A. Primary sources provide first-hand information about events or occurrences and include sources like speeches, government and legal documents, photographs, and more. They are usually strong evidence.

4)

A. Competition in business is an aspect of the market economy.

5)

C. Anthropology—the study of people—requires interacting with the groups under investigation.

6)

D. Geography studies space; the physical space of the earth; and the ways in which it interacts with, shapes, and is shaped by its habitants.

7)

C. When re-teaching a concept, the teacher should break down what confused students don't understand and restate learning targets and learning objectives.

8)

D. A Venn diagram can help students identify a given topic's similarities and differences.

9)

B. An analytic rubric assesses a student's understanding of more detailed skills, in this case appropriate vocabulary.

10)

A. A multiple-choice test would quickly assess student understanding of content knowledge.

11)

B. This question asks students to form their own opinions based on their knowledge of inventions during the Industrial Revolution and their contributions to society.

12)

B. It is the researcher's responsibility to ensure credibility and contemporaneity of sources; it is essential for teachers to ensure that students understand this.

→ Go on

13)

A.   This lesson examines the consequences of interpersonal behaviors in school.

14)

D.   Studying candidates and issues helps students understand how to vote responsibly.

Follow the link below to take your second TExES History 7 – 12 (233) practice test and to access other online study resources:

www.cirrustestprep.com/texes-history-online-resources